The

Also by Christine Pullein-Thompson
in Dragon Books

THE FIRST ROSETTE
FOR WANT OF A SADDLE
IMPOSSIBLE HORSE
THE SECOND MOUNT
THE EMPTY FIELD
THREE TO RIDE
THE PONY DOPERS
THE LOST PONY
PONY PATROL S.O.S.

Christine Pullein-Thompson

The Open Gate

Illustrated

DRAGON
GRANADA PUBLISHING
London Toronto Sydney New York

Published by Granada Publishing Limited
in Dragon Books 1967
Reprinted 1970, 1975, 1978

ISBN 0 583 30060 X

First published in Great Britain by
Burke Publishing Co Ltd 1962
This edition first published by
Atlantic Publishing Co Ltd 1967

Granada Publishing Limited
Frogmore, St Albans, Herts AL2 2NF
and
3 Upper James Street, London W1R 4BP
1221 Avenue of the Americas, New York, NY 10020, USA
117 York Street, Sydney, NSW 2000, Australia
100 Skyway Avenue, Toronto, Ontario, Canada M9W 3A6
110 Northpark Centre, 2193 Johannesburg, South Africa
CML Centre, Queen & Wyndham, Auckland 1, New Zealand

Made and printed in Great Britain by
C. Nicholls & Company Ltd
The Philips Park Press, Manchester
Set in Intertype Times

"What Can Have Happened?"

It was summer again. The visitors were back by the seashore; every pony was booked for weeks ahead at the riding-school. The slag-heaps hadn't changed – they still raised the same dusty, forgotten heads to the sky.

The gang at the riding-school were a year older; older and wiser; otherwise the same.

On the first morning of the summer holidays Stella arrived first. As she got off the seven o'clock bus, she thought, "No more school for six weeks." And that meant six weeks of helping at Miss Lewis's riding-school, since her mother was a widow and was out all day at work.

Stella had short, straight hair, and a nose which turned up at the end. She rode officially once a week; but countless other times, bareback to fields, to the blacksmith, or when pupils cancelled their booking and a pony was free. Now she could see Jocelyn and James Allcott coming towards her along the road.

"Look, there's Stella. We're not first after all," dark-haired James said to his sister. He started to run. "I want to be first," he called back over his shoulder.

"And that's James all over," decided Jocelyn, who wore spectacles and had her chestnut hair cut short. She was neat and orderly. Whatever she did, her hair stayed tidy and her hands clean. She didn't run after her brother now, but walked, thinking, "After all we were here last Saturday. It's not as though we've been away for months, and it's not our turn for a ride even if there is a cancellation."

Audrey Lewis was mucking out when the children reached the yard. "Would you like to collect the ponies from the bottom meadow?" she called. "You'll find halters in the saddle-room."

"Okay. Bags ride Patchwork," replied Stella.

The three Fisher girls were arguing as they ran along the road.

"It is my turn because you had the last free ride last holidays," shouted Maria. "I know it is . . ."

"Don't shout so. The whole district will hear you," replied Anne, who often wished she came from a more ordinary family – for their father was an artist, and their mother unusual to look at, with her long hair and her fringe.

Bromwyn, the eldest, had lapsed into a dream. She had brought sketching materials with her. For weeks now she had been planning to paint the stable-yard; all through the long summer term she had been waiting for the day to arrive when she could sit trying to catch the light and shade, the frenzied activity, the individuality of the ponies, the whole feeling of the Seashore School of Equitation. Now that the morning had come, she suddenly had cold feet. "I've taken on too much," she thought. "I'm simply not good enough . . . . I can't do it, I know I can't."

The Fisher girls all had the same dark hair and blue eyes. They wore faded shirts, plimsolls and well-worn jodhpurs. Lately, their father had held a successful exhibition in New York, so that now the cottage where they lived was being enlarged and done up; the kitchen was perpetually full of workmen; Bromwyn's bedroom had disappeared altogether to emerge later as part of a guest-room; and the three girls had suddenly discovered that they were to have a sitting-room to themselves.

"Well, anyway I don't suppose we'll be offered a ride," Anne said, as they entered the yard. "Look, the Allcotts and Stella have raced us."

"We've bagged ride back Patchwork, Dawn and Turpin," James called, waving a halter.

"Can I leave my sketching things in the saddle-room, Audrey?" asked Anne.

Ivor helped his mother to finish the washing up. "There you are, Mum. Want anything from the village? I'm going to the riding-school now...."

His father had left for the mine wearing his working clothes, his cap and his thick boots. He could hear his sister moving about upstairs. In a minute she would be coming down to hurry along the road past the terrace houses to catch the bus into town where she worked as a hairdresser.

"You might get some mince from the butcher on the way home," his mother said.

Ivor took the last cup off the oil-cloth and put it in the cupboard. Once he was outside he could smell the sea. He started to run, recalling that last summer he and the gang of helpers at the riding-school had saved three Shire horses from Irish slaughter-houses, or worse still, French ones. "I'd like to do something like that again," he thought. "Last summer was the best summer of my life." Now it was all over he couldn't remember the bad bits, only the sweet, heady feeling of success.

"Just in time," called Anne Fisher when he reached the stables. "We thought you might come."

"Hullo Ivor," called Audrey.

He felt at home here; sometimes more so than in the terrace house where he lived. His sister would tease him, "Why you want to work with smelly animals, Ivor, beats me. Honest it does. There's no future in it... now hairdressing, well that's a trade..." she would say, looking at her varnished nails.

"That's no trade, that's nothing. Just a dead end." he said once, and that had caused a real rumpus.

But now everybody knew that he meant to be a jockey. He had made contact with a racing stable, thanks to Audrey, and before long he would be leaving, perhaps next year, perhaps the one after.

"Thanks for waiting," he said.

"That's all right."

The seven of them set off along the road towards the bottom meadow. "Is Dobbin all right?" Ivor asked, for they still had the grey Shire horse left.

"Yes. We've been asked to take her to the Church Fête," James said. "It will mean washing her and plaiting her mane and everything. I thought she could carry a box for our *Save the Horses in Ireland Fund*. We haven't a penny towards it now."

"No, nothing at all," agreed Jocelyn.

It was like a thousand other mornings. Gulls wheeled in the sky; the fishing-boats were coming in; the sun was appearing through haze, promising a fine day; it was like so many other mornings which the children carried with them in their minds. How often before they had walked together along the narrow road, partly obscured by high hedges; then on past the new bungalows, where alarm clocks were ringing, where curtains were still drawn, and milk bottles already delivered outside the glistening, new back doors.

"Ugh," exclaimed Bromwyn, turning her eyes away.

"What's wrong? Better than back-to-back houses, aren't they?" asked Ivor.

""I like the really modern stuff; all glass and swimming-pool," said James.

They turned down the track which led to the bottom meadow. There were still dewy cobwebs on the bramble bushes on each side.

"I should like to live in rooms above stables; looking across a yard to a clock set in an arch. A real old-fashioned stable-yard," said Stella who lived in a flat sharing the bathroom with the family below.

"It looks as though some motor-bikes have been down here," remarked James.

"And the gate's open!" shouted Maria, as they turned the last corner. "Look!"

They stopped for a moment and stared.

"The ponies may still be there," said Jocelyn.

"*May* is the word," exclaimed Bromwyn.

They started to run.

"But it's always chained," said Jocelyn.

"Exactly," agreed Anne.

"Oh dear," said Maria.

Ivor had a choking sensation in his throat. "Supposing Patchwork is hurt? The ponies could have reached the railway-line, and been sliced to pieces by a train. But then we would have heard, surely we would have heard; Dad would have been told at the men's club, or Mum when she popped round the corner to the shop," he thought. But the choking sensation stayed.

"Supposing we can't find them? The pupils will come just the same. What will Audrey do?" wondered Jocelyn; while James was puzzled about what the tyre marks meant and why motor-bikes should come down a rough, deserted lane.

They reached the field and Maria shouted, "Turpin's here. Look!"

"Hurray!" said James.

"And Frosty. But where are the others ...?" Jocelyn asked.

"Perhaps they're under the trees," Bromwyn said, trying to stay calm.

The bottom meadow ran slightly downhill to a stream and the railway-line.

The two ponies were by the stream. They stood still, each resting a hind leg; but their heads were up, and when they saw the children they started to trot away.

"There's a lemonade bottle by the gate," Jocelyn said.

"Where can the other ponies be?" asked Maria. "The person who left the gate open should be shot."

"I've looked in the diary. Every pony is booked for the ten o'clock ride," James said.

"The first day of the holidays and this happens," exclaimed Bromwyn, who could see her morning painting disappearing into one of anxious searching.

"We had better look on the line," suggested Ivor gloomily.

"But the gate's open," Jocelyn said.

"Let's have a look at Frosty and Turpin. Why are *they* here and not the others?" asked Anne.

They shut the gate behind them. The ponies were trotting round the field; the grass was wet with dew, and the sun was lighting everything with the light of summer.

"How many ponies should there be here?" asked James.

"Seven, of course," said his sister.

"Look, Turpin is caked with mud and sweat, and his mouth is bleeding. Look!" shouted Maria, beginning to run.

"Don't run," shouted everybody.

"What can have happened?" asked Anne.

"I don't know, but I can guess," James answered.

"Poor Turpin, poor little Turpin," Stella said.

"Poor Frosty. Look, there's blood on his legs," shouted Maria.

"What are we going to do?" asked Ivor.

"Whoa, little horses. Whoa," said James, and thought of the tyre marks on the track outside the field. "This could be the beginning of something," he decided; "could even lead to the end of the riding-school.

"Two of us had better catch the ponies here and the

rest go in search of the others," he said.

"Right you are," exclaimed Anne.

"Bags stay," said Stella.

"I'll keep you company," Maria said.

The two girls stood talking to the ponies, holding oats in one hand, and halters in the other, hidden behind their backs.

"Where do we go from here?" Anne asked. "Shall I go to the stable and give the alarm?"

"Good idea," James replied.

Ivor was still imagining Patchwork dead on the railway-line. "I hate motor-bikes; always have done," he said, as they climbed the field gate.

They stopped to look at the marks in the trampled grass. James turned over an empty cigarette packet with his foot. Bromwyn found cigarette ends tinted with lipstick. Jocelyn kicked a broken bottle into a pile of brambles.

Ivor said, "It looks as though half a dozen bikes have been down here."

There was a stream of cars on the road when they reached it.

"What now?" asked Bromwyn, and now she knew that once again she wouldn't paint. The dew had come through her plimsolls. "The workmen will be turning up at home," she thought; "will the cottage ever be in order again?"

"We had better split up. Anyone coming?" Ivor asked. "We should have brought a dog," he thought. "Dad's dog would have done." He started to run, and Jocelyn ran with him, her spectacles suddenly misty with tears as she thought, "Supposing he's right? Supposing they are dead on the line?"

"Good-bye all. I'll tell Audrey; and good luck," Anne said, walking purposefully towards the riding-school. She was thinking, "The others are panicking, the ponies will turn up all right."

"I'm going to town. Coming Bromwyn? We might call at the police station on the way. I fear the worst," said James, and suddenly he was running, his heart pounding against his ribs; voices and the splash of peaceful waves came to him from the beach.

"The police! Isn't it rather early to go to the police?" Bromwyn asked.

"It's never too early," James replied.

"I've never cared for them myself," Bromwyn said.

"You must be mad then," retorted James, and now he could see the constable's neat, modern house, and the flowers which grew beneath the windows.

"The police are there to help," he said, and knew suddenly that his father had said that to him long ago.

"But what will Audrey say? Shouldn't we ask her first? After all, the police may take her up for letting her ponies stray. What then? I'm sure we should wait."

"You can if you like. I'm not going to," James answered.

"But what will the police do?"

"They may have been rung up. People do tell them if they find animals straying."

He opened the constable's gate. In the next-door garden a dog barked. He could hear a baby crying. From the house came the smell of bacon and eggs.

"I'm sure we shouldn't be doing this," Bromwyn said.

"Go back if you like," retorted James, his finger finding a bell. "I know I'm right," he thought. "Last time we nearly waited too long, if Nicholas hadn't gone to the police . . ." he could hear feet coming towards the door.

"Be quiet, Mark," a woman's voice said then, "What is it?" as she opened the door.

Ivor and Jocelyn had reached the golf-links. Voices shouted, "Ball," and "I say, well putted."

"Keep off the greens," Jocelyn said.

"What do you think I'm doing—" Ivor retorted, and wished that Maria was with him, instead of slow, methodical, tidy Jocelyn Allcott. Presently they could see the railway-line, and away to the left the sea. The sand wasn't crowded yet. Early risers were still walking their dogs, and a few enthusiastic children were digging castles; a man in shorts stood throwing driftwood at the sea.

"Let's look for hoof-marks" suggested Jocelyn.

"Isn't the ground too hard?" asked Ivor. "I'm going on down to the railway-line. There may be a clue there. After all this golf-course is open. There's not many places the ponies can have got to."

"What have the motor-bikes got to do with it all?"

"I suppose the riders left the gate open."

"And threw stones at Turpin and Frosty?"

"I don't know. It's a mystery, isn't it?"

A goods train was moving slowly along the line, leaving a stream of thick, dirty smoke in its wake.

The children could see golfers swinging clubs and could hear the sharp rap of club against ball.

They started to run, ignoring a notice which read, *Golfers only*.

"What will Audrey say? What will she do?" wondered Ivor. "I wonder if Mum's heard anything yet. She hears most things."

Jocelyn was behind now. She stopped to wipe her spectacles. "The ponies are probably safe in a farmer's field. People are pretty decent really," she thought.

Frosty and Turpin walked up to the two girls at last. "Look, Frosty's shoe's half off; that puts him out of use until he goes to the blacksmith," Stella said.

"And his leg's cut too. It could be an overreach.

Perhaps he ought to have an anti-tetanus injection," Maria said.

Then they started to examine small, black Turpin who was old and kind and who had taught hundreds of children to ride, so that he was remembered in many parts of the world by people just grown up, who were grateful to him for their introduction to riding.

He looked very old this morning, and Maria thought she could detect a hurt look in his eyes. One side of his mouth was sore, and his round, black sides were caked with dried sweat.

"Come on, we'd better get them both to the stables as quick as we can," Stella said.

"Yes. How awful it is. Poor old Turpin! It's the work of a gang, isn't it? I know it is. Poor little Turpin," Maria said.

But Frosty wouldn't hurry; and Turpin seemed to imagine enemies hidden in every bramble and shadow. The road was thick with traffic to the town when they reached it, so that they both knew that soon it would be nine o'clock.

"What will Audrey say?" wondered Stella.

"What about the pupils?" asked Maria.

"They just won't be able to ride."

"That's pretty obvious, isn't it?"

"Someone's coming down the road to meet us."

Anne was panting when she reached the stable-yard. Audrey had finished mucking out. Her dogs were sunning themselves. Suddenly, Anne saw how humble the yard was really – just seven shabby loose-boxes, an open shed, saddle-room and granary and Audrey's own small-windowed cottage. Two guinea fowls were scratching by the oat-bin. A cat lay purring on a horse-rug.

"Audrey, Audrey. Catastrophe," cried Anne. In a moment, the peace of the yard was shattered. The dogs sat up; the cat stopped purring, and the guinea fowls ran squawking across the paddock, where the battered jumps awaited the ten o'clock class.

"What is it? Where are the ponies?" asked Audrey, appearing from the saddle-room, with her arms full of tack.

"They've got out, except for Frosty and Turpin who are half scared out of their wits."

"Oh no," Audrey said, "But how?"

Anne started to explain. "The motor-bikes must have frightened them or something," she finished.

"But why should motor-bikes want to go down there?" asked Audrey.

"Perhaps for a midnight picnic or something," suggested Anne.

"It sounds improbable. Why not the golf-links or the beach?"

"The others are looking for them. How can I help?" Anne asked.

"I don't know," said Audrey. "Pupils will be turning up soon. Oh dear . . . Perhaps we'd better go to the gate and see if anyone's had any luck. The ponies can't have gone far."

"Why hasn't any one seen them? It seems so peculiar," Anne replied as they whistled to the dogs and hurried along the road, with their eyes screwed up against the morning sun.

Nicholas Arrives

Nicholas was saddling his grey mare, Trombone. He had arrived home from school the previous day; because of that he was still seeing the Victorian house where he lived with his parents as if for the first time. It was always like that when he came home; each holidays the house would seem a little smaller, though it was large enough, with five bedrooms, and had seemed a mansion to him at the age of five.

Trombone had been pleased to see him. His father's boxer, Watchman, had greeted him with a succession of short, excited barks. There had been his favourite cake for tea; and salmon for dinner in the high-ceilinged dining-room. He had found a list of Pony Club activities in his bedroom. He had great plans for Trombone during the summer; he always had great plans for her but very often they came to nothing.

At breakfast his mother had said, "You're going to the riding-school as usual, I suppose," and he had nodded, and wondered how many of the old gang would be there. Bromwyn had written to him during the holidays. He wondered whether she would be wearing the same old clothes, or whether sudden success had changed Mr. Fisher, making him more generous to his three daughters.

Nicholas waved to his mother as he rode down the short drive to the road. It was still early; a boy was delivering papers, and a postman was carrying a bag of mail into the hotel at the top of the hill before the village. The hotel was new, with large plate-glass windows. Nicholas hated it. He took the short cut to the stables, riding across fields which had recently been scheduled for building land. "Next holidays I shall be riding past bungalows, I expect," he thought; "the fields will have gone."

He pushed Trombone into a canter and could see the sea breaking calmly on almost deserted beaches. Sea air stung his face; familiar, half-forgotten smells came back to him. He reached the road, trotted into the stable-yard. "Hullo, hullo," he called.

He waited, expecting a welcome; but even the dogs were absent.

"Whatever's happened, Trombone?" he asked, dis-

Sea air stung his face

mounting. "Where's the gang? Where's Audrey? Where's everybody?"

Tall, fair-headed, broad-shouldered, self-possessed, he walked round the yard looking into the loose-boxes.

"It's all most peculiar," he said to the mare. "Where is everybody?"

Then the telephone rang in the saddle-room. After tying up Trombone, he answered it. But it was only a parent calling, wishing to know whether her daughter Rosemary was booked for the ten o'clock ride. He checked the list in the diary and her name was there. "Yes, that's all right," he said. Putting down the diary he stepped outside in time to see Audrey, Maria and Stella leading Frosty and Turpin into the yard. "I say, what's happened?" he called.

They started to explain, at least the girls did, while Audrey paced the yard and her two dogs sat eyeing her with anxious faces.

"You say the gate was open, and the chain's gone. It sounds like a case for the police," announced Nicholas.

"James has already gone, I think," Stella said. "He went that way, anyway."

"I'll look for them on Trombone," Nicholas said. "They can't be far. It seems funny they didn't come here."

"They always have before," Audrey replied. "The pupils will be here soon. I really don't know what I'm going to do. Frosty and Turpin don't look fit for work. It's not as though the pupils are regular ones. They are nearly all visitors whose rides were booked by their hotels. If I can't take them I will lose a lot of goodwill."

"But it's not your fault," cried Maria.

There was a note of hysteria in their voices; but then, Nicholas recollected, Maria always was inclined to panic. He was different. He believed he had the ability to keep his head, as his father had done in two world wars.

"We'll find them. Come on, Trombone," he said mounting, and then riding out into the sunlit road.

"Is there anything to do? What about the grooming?" asked Maria, pushing her long, dark hair back from her face.

"You can groom Rocket if you like. I've done the others," Audrey said, wringing her worn hands together.

"When will this morning's pupils start to arrive," wondered Maria. "Surely the others will find the missing ponies soon."

Audrey fetched some antiseptic and started to bathe Frosty's leg. Presently she said, "He'll need an anti-tetanus injection. I'd better ring the vet."

"Oh dear, I'm sorry," said Maria. She continued grooming dark brown Rocket, who had been giving rides on a beach when Audrey found him. Stella was silently grooming Northwind, a grey gelding of fourteen hands. She had these fits of silence, probably because she was often alone.

"Nicholas hardly said hullo," she thought. "He's grown. He looks almost grown up." Then she exclaimed, "Stand still, Northwind and don't bite," as she saw a Bentley stopping outside. Two girls got out.

Stella ran out of the loose-box, but the Bentley had gone. The two girls came up the drive, immaculately dressed in well-cut fawn jodhpurs, checked jackets, riding-sticks in their hands. They looked too well-dressed to be true, like dummies in a shop window.

"Who are we riding?" they called. "Last year it was Frosty and Dawn."

Stella could hear Audrey telephoning in the saddle-room. "Yes. It looks like a wire cut; it's jagged, and there's a large flap to it. Yes, just the wound for breeding tetanus." She came out of the saddle-room and stood staring at the two children.

"Hullo, Miss Lewis, you do remember us, don't you?" they said. "We rode last year. Diana and Stephanie Thompson. We rode Frosty and Dawn. Do you think we've outgrown Dawn?"

"What can I do for you?" asked Constable Wilson's wife. "Oh, here's my husband."

"We've come about some ponies," James said.

"About Miss Lewis's. Someone's let them out. We thought you might have heard something," Bromwyn said.

A cat purred against the constable's legs.

"No, I've heard nothing. Let me take some particulars," he said. "How many are missing? Where were they?"

The children started to explain.

"Of course, they may have heard something at the Station in the town. I'll put a call through," Constable Wilson said, when the explaining was done. "Just step inside," he added. They sat down in armchairs.

"I meant to go home for breakfast. I'm getting hungry," James exclaimed.

"The smell of bacon and eggs doesn't exactly help, does it?" asked Bromwyn.

"All this seems an awful waste of time," James muttered, and Bromwyn suddenly saw that he was like his father in many ways, with the same air of weary impatience.

The cat jumped on to Bromwyn's knee. "I like short-haired cats best," she said.

Then Constable Wilson came back.

"No luck there either. But they'll let the patrol car know; and if there's any news, well, we'll ring Miss Lewis."

"What about the motor-bikes? Have any gangs been seen about?" asked James, standing up.

"I wouldn't know about that. But you mustn't jump to conclusions," the constable said. "I'll be looking out for Miss Lewis's ponies, don't you worry."

"But what about the two which got left behind? How did they get hurt? They were covered with dry sweat," James asked.

"Well, you know how it is. Perhaps they couldn't find the gate in the dark, were galloping up and down, got into some wire. Horses are nervous creatures, you know," the constable said.

"I don't know."

"There doesn't seem much point in going to the town. The police would know if they had been that way," Bromwyn said, walking down the garden path. "He's not very clever, is he?" she added.

"You've got a down on the police anyway," James retorted, though he was disappointed too. "Perhaps we'd better go back to the stables. Someone may have telephoned, or Ivor and Jocelyn may have had better luck."

"I wonder if Nicholas is home yet," Bromwyn said, and James remembered that she had always been keen on Nicholas.

There were cars going down to the beach now; and the road and the bungalows they passed all seemed to have a holiday feeling about them. Bathing-dresses hung on clothes-lines, and buckets and spades were stacked neatly outside a front door.

"Audrey stands to lose a lot of money if we don't find the ponies. She charges eight and six an hour, and there'll be seven ponies out of action for three hours today. How much does that make?"

"I can't do arithmetic in the early morning," Bromwyn replied.

"It's fifty-six shillings three times, plus the sixpences. That must be two pounds nineteen and six three times – eight pounds eighteen and sixpence," James said triumphantly. "Think of that, nearly nine pounds. I would be raving mad if I was Audrey."

"Well, you're not and she doesn't care about money. She'll be worrying about the ponies," Bromwyn said.

"Surely they can't all be hurt?" James said.

"Perhaps they're dead. Perhaps madmen rode them into the sea. Perhaps they've been put into trucks and smuggled to the abattoirs of France on the night ferry. All sorts of things happen nowadays which ordinary people never hear about," said Bromwyn. "Come on, let's run. I feel better when we run; I feel that at least we're *trying* to do something to help."

"Well, we are, aren't we? We've been to the police, and they've rung the main police station, or whatever it's called, and the patrol cars are on the look out. We've done a lot, haven't we? More than all the others put together if you ask me," James said.

"Well, I don't."

"Don't what?"

"Ask you."

The sun was hot now; but the two children could see clouds gathering in the north, so that James thought, "It'll rain soon," and Bromwyn decided that the whole day was doomed so far as her painting was concerned. They could see the stable-yard now; the rusting corrugated roofs of the loose-boxes, the single chimney of Audrey's cottage, from which no smoke came.

They broke into a walk and, as they did so, an Austin stopped outside the riding-school and two people in beach clothes, a large boy with glasses and a small fair girl with pigtails started to walk up the drive.

"Oh goodness, poor Audrey," exclaimed Bromwyn.

"What will she do?" wondered James, thinking again, "Eight pounds, eighteen shillings and sixpence. Enough to buy quite a good railway set; it's a lot of money to lose."

"There's nothing on the railway-line," said Jocelyn panting after Ivor. "Look, the wire isn't broken. Anyway what pony could get down the embankment?"

The goods train had gone, to be followed by a tearing passenger train bringing still more visitors to the seaside town. Ivor could see some of them leaning out of windows, smelling the air. As the train neared the town it hooted wildly.

"Yes, we'd better turn back," Ivor said. He could hear golfers talking about hotels and breakfasts.

"It's the ketchup I can't stand," said one.

"I don't mind that so much. It's the service which drives me round the bend . . ." said another.

"And what's wrong with ketchup?" wondered Ivor. They could see the sea again, Smuggler's Cove and the sand-dunes. They turned their backs on it and started to walk disconsolately back across the golf-links. Fresh golfers were leaving the club-house; a caddy carried clubs.

"I can't think what's happened to the ponies, can you, Jocelyn?" Ivor asked.

He was worrying now. "But then who wouldn't?" he asked himself. Everybody knew what teenagers were like on motor-bikes. He had seen them roaring through the narrow streets among the shabby terrace houses, frightening the dogs, sending the cats scuttling over fences, and the little children running to their mothers.

"It shouldn't be allowed," his mother had said, over and over again. "They'll kill someone before they've finished or kill themselves." But Ivor hadn't agreed.

"It's like racing, I expect," he had argued. "Racing horses I mean."

"I know what you mean. But race-horses only go forty miles an hour; these fools go through the streets at eighty," his mother had answered.

And one day one *had* crashed and had been taken away by ambulance. Half the street had watched him go; but the bikes still came roaring through the street at weekends, revving up their engines, very often with girls sitting behind the boys.

"I don't know what to think," Jocelyn said.

"The motor-bikes had something to do with it. You can bet on that," Ivor said.

There seemed no point in running. Either the other children had found the ponies, or the ponies were miles away, or that's how Ivor reckoned it. And when the ponies were found who could tell how they would look. Perhaps small piebald Patchwork was lamed for life. "If I could get hold of those teenagers I would shake them till their teeth rattled," decided Ivor.

"Jubilee's Missing"

They were all back at the stables now, including Nicholas. The four pupils who had come ready for their rides had decided to stay. The boy with spectacles was called Daniel.

"But you can call me Dan if you like," he told everyone.

Audrey had telephoned the police station in the town. Now the vet had arrived. "Where's the pony?" he asked, and then, "Poor little thing, what a wound," he said.

"Let's go to the granary," Bromwyn suggested. "We can discuss things there."

They hurried there – Jocelyn and James, the three Fisher girls, and Ivor, Nicholas and Stella; Daniel joined them, though no one had asked him.

The sat on bales of straw and Nicholas said, "Well,

suggestions please. I haven't seen the scene of the crime you know."

"Audrey doesn't think teenagers have anything to do with it," said Anne.

"Nor do the police. But they are often wrong anyway," said Bromwyn.

"Audrey never thinks badly of anyone," observed Nicholas.

"No, they could skin her alive and she would still say it was a mistake and they hadn't meant to," agreed Bromwyn.

"Frosty and Turpin look as though they've been ridden; that's the evidence, that and the tyre marks," James said.

"Listen, the telephone's ringing," Ivor exclaimed.

"There are more pupils coming. Look, a crowd of them off the ten o'clock bus," observed Stella who knew all the buses by heart because she so often travelled on them.

"The ponies are found," called Audrey. "They're at Hillsbridge."

"But that's nearly ten miles away," cried Nicholas.

They scrambled out of the granary. "If I take you over in my car, will you bring them back for me?" Audrey asked.

"Yes."

"Yes, of course."

"Can we ring up Mummy and Daddy first?" asked James.

"Can I come with you?" asked Daniel.

In the end they couldn't all go, for there simply wasn't room in Audrey's small, battered car. Nicholas offered to stay, saying he would meet them on Trombone; Jocelyn decided to go home to help her mother, because a new paying-guest was expected in the modern bungalow where the Allcotts lived.

So Daniel, Stella, Ivor, Bromwyn, Maria, James

and Anne crowded into the car. Audrey started the engine and they set off for Hillsbridge, the dogs watching their departure with mournful eyes.

"Are some of you coming back with me? There seem rather a lot of you for five ponies," observed Audrey.

"Perhaps I should. I mean, I'm the newcomer, aren't I?" asked Daniel.

None of them could pretend that they liked Daniel; they resented his company, because Jocelyn had had to give up her place in the car to him.

The road to Hillsbridge was crowded with holiday-makers. They were very hot in the car and there wasn't room to move much. Audrey was too worried for conversation. Ivor could only wonder how Patchwork would be when they found him. James wondered what his mother would say when he eventually returned home; only yesterday she had made a new rule.

She had stood in the sitting-room with her back to the television set and had said, "Now listen to me, James and Jocelyn, please, just for one minute. I have no objection to you going to the riding-school in the holidays. I like you to enjoy yourselves. But I must insist that you return for at least some meals. I don't like you going without a cooked breakfast; if you're having sandwiches for lunch you must be here for breakfast; is that understood?"

She had said a lot more about meals; James couldn't remember it all because he hadn't really listened once he had caught the gist of it. And now here he was on the first morning of the holidays missing a cooked breakfast, and he would probably miss lunch as well. He wished now that he had gone back with Jocelyn to help prepare the bungalow for the paying-guest, an elderly lady with arthritis.

Bromwyn was thinking about her paints and canvas left in the stable-yard. Supposing it rained? "But then something always does happen to stop me painting," she thought; "last summer it was the horses we had to save from Jim Morgan and the slaughter-houses, and this summer I suppose it will be something else."

Anne was thinking of the long journey back. They might have to take it in turns to walk. How on earth had the ponies got to Hillsbridge, she wondered. Stella remembered that she had promised to catch the one-thirty bus home. Her mother had asked her to do some shopping. "It will be so much easier if I don't have to do it on the way home," her mother had said.

Maria was thinking about people on motor-bikes. Her father hated them; but then he didn't like cars either, or planes. If he went anywhere he walked to the station and then caught a train, and if he did take a taxi it had to be one of the high, old-fashioned ones.

Daniel kept looking at the other occupants of the car. They fascinated him. They were entirely different from the rather stuffy well-brought up children in the hotel where he was staying. "They're such a mixture," he thought, looking from Ivor to Bromwyn and back again. "Horsy people are the oddest in the world. They don't run true to type; there isn't a type at all."

But now they had reached Hillsbridge. "They're at Stambrokeshire Farm," Audrey said in a weary voice as she turned the car down a stony lane.

"How did the police find them?" Stella asked.

"The farmer telephoned; no doubt he was surprised to find so many ponies in his field."

"Are the police looking for the culprits?" asked Bromwyn.

"What culprits?"

"The people who brought the ponies here."

"Perhaps they came here of their own accord," Audrey answered.

Nobody liked to contradict her.

"What a beautiful place," Daniel said, and they all

climbed out and stood looking at the homely little farm with its whitewashed buildings.

"But where are the ponies?" asked Maria.

A farmhand appeared. "You've come for the ponies I expect," he said.

Their hearts sank. Ivor imagined Patchwork limping painfully, his tendon severed. "That will mean the humane killer," he thought.

"Any sign of motor-bikes round here?" James asked.

"Funny thing you should ask that. There were tyre marks by the gate this morning," the man said.

James couldn't help his spirits rising, because he knew suddenly that he was on the right track. At the same time he was afraid too. "They'll come again as likely as not," he thought.

"They're down the bottom of the field. One of them is lying down," said the man, opening the gate.

"I should be back at the stables; but I'd better see the worst first," Audrey said.

Maria wanted to run ahead of them all; Ivor found himself twisting his hands together. Audrey started to call the ponies; but none of them came; there wasn't a single whinny.

"What's this about motor-bikes?" Daniel wanted to know.

But none of them answered him. They crossed a tinkling stream, and now they could see the ponies standing together in a group, their heads hanging.

"Gosh, they look tired," exclaimed James.

"Patchwork's lying down," shouted Ivor, staring at the piebald pony, which looked like a little china ornament placed on a green chimneypiece. Now Dawn whinnied, raising her neat grey head, and they saw that chestnut Firecracker was resting a foreleg. Tango, a black pony, walked towards them.

"Jubilee's missing," Audrey said.

And they all stood looking at the ponies wondering where Jubilee was.

Then Audrey walked up to Patchwork. The piebald pony stood up and they saw that his mouth was sore at each corner and his knees were broken. For an awful second everyone thought Audrey would cry. They all looked away tactfully, but her face hardly changed. "Poor little Patchwork," she said.

"I knew all along he was hurt," exclaimed Ivor.

"We'll have to send a horsebox for him," Audrey said and they all knew that was another expense on top of the money she had lost during the morning.

She started to examine Firecracker. "He's wrenched his shoulder; he had better go by box too. You can lead or ride the others back if you like," she said.

"That leaves two. What are we going to do about Jubilee?" Bromwyn asked.

"I'll stay and look for her," James answered.

"You know you can't. What would your mother say?" asked Audrey.

And James knew suddenly that he couldn't.

"But *I* can. Mum doesn't mind what time I get in. She says I'm like a bad penny – I always turn up," Ivor said.

"You can wait for the horsebox then," Audrey said.

"I'll stay too. I'm so late already, a few more hours won't matter much," Stella said, and she knew how it would be in the evening, how her mother would say, "Oh Stella, how could you not do the shopping?" And then a moment later, "Oh well, we'll have to eat out of tins again . . ."

"I'd better come back with you, Miss Lewis. I mustn't miss luncheon," Daniel said.

"Will you come with me too, Anne? I shall need someone to answer the telephone," Audrey asked.

"There's only Dawn and Tango, so I will come with

you too. Perhaps I can borrow a bike and search for Jubilee later," Bromwyn suggested.

"So that leaves us two," James said to Maria.

"I'll lead Tango," Maria said.

"You must ride some of the way. I won't have you walking ten miles. What would your mother say?" asked Audrey.

They put bridles on the two ponies. Audrey, Anne, Bromwyn and Daniel walked back to the car.

"Why on earth did Daniel want to come?" asked Maria.

"Perhaps he doesn't like his posh hotel," James suggested. They said good-bye to Stella and Ivor.

"Dawn's been ridden all right. Any fool can see that. Why's Audrey pretending to be blind?" James asked.

"I don't know. But I feel like yelling at every motor-bike I see. What beasts they must be," Maria shouted.

"What, the bikes or their riders?"

"You know what I mean."

"Don't let's quarrel, we've got ten miles in front of us," James said.

"Poor Audrey, it's going to be an awful expense," Maria said.

"If it goes on she'll have to give up. You know that, don't you?" James asked.

They were silent after that, each thinking of the holidays without Audrey and the riding-school.

They rode the ponies at first; and all the time clouds were gathering in the sky, so they knew that soon it would rain and most likely they would arrive home soaked to the skin. James knew the reception he would get then; and he couldn't blame his mother, for the bungalow was small, with the airing-cupboard in the kitchen. And, of course, the new paying-guest would have arrived, making more work for Mrs. Allcott. He started to feel very gloomy. Dawn stumbled for the third time and he dismounted; at the same moment the rain started.

"Oh, goodness," exclaimed Maria, "and we've still got eight miles ahead of us."

"It's going to rain," Ivor said to Stella as they stood by the two lame ponies. "How long will it take for the horsebox to get here, do you suppose?"

"About an hour."

"Or two hours or three," said Ivor.

"You are gloomy, aren't you?"

"Well, look at the ponies. Just look at them. Poor little Patchwork who never hurt anyone. Look at her mouth; and her knees will be scarred for ever, most likely. She'll never win any more prizes for Audrey, that's certain. And Firecracker, look at him . . ."

"Well, what can we do?" asked Stella.

"Plenty. I'm not sitting back and doing nothing, whatever Audrey says," answered Ivor.

"Try To Climb Out"

Riding Trombone towards Hillsbridge, Nicholas decided that, as usual, James was making a fuss about nothing. "More likely Audrey's right," he thought; "probably the ponies just got out and wandered. James always has been one for melodrama."

Trombone had been turned out for three months so he couldn't ride very fast. Though there were clouds gathering, the sun was still hot, and presently she was sweating. As usual everywhere was crowded with holiday-makers; cars crawled in a long column towards the sea; coaches disgorged a crowd of travellers outside a café.

"I shall emigrate when I'm old enough," Nicholas decided. "Britain's getting impossible." He could hear a pony whinnying. On each side of him were woods, but above the trees he could see the tops of slag-heaps, and beyond them was the railway-line.

Nicholas looked at his watch. Ten-fifteen. How many pupils had collected at the riding-school, he wondered. He was sorry for Audrey. The whinny came again and Trombone raised her head and neighed. "Come on, we can't stop and talk to every horse who neighs," Nicholas said, for the grey mare had stopped; and the whinny came again, more urgent this time, like a desperate call for help.

"It's from the wood," Nicholas decided. "Why should anybody leave a pony in a wood?" he wondered, before he saw that the fence was broken. Nicholas looked at the gap for some time before he rode through it into the wood. Almost at once he came upon a heap of old bottles, and saw bits of paper were strewn everywhere. It was the sort of wood he hated – a mass of tangled undergrowth, stunted trees and derelict paths, with a background of old slag-heaps.

The pony was whinnying again now; clouds were gathering in the sky, and Nicholas was afraid he would miss the others who were coming home with the ponies which had strayed. "What an awful beginning to the holidays," he thought, guiding Trombone round the heap of bottles. He found a derelict path and here there were hoofprints, and the bracken was trampled where it had grown across the path. The whinny sounded near when the pony called again, but Nicholas still couldn't see where it came from.

"How mysterious it is," he thought; then Trombone swung off the path, her grey ears pricked. "I suppose you know what you're doing," Nicholas said, before he saw the pit with Jubilee at the bottom of it.

"Whatever shall I do?" he wondered, dismounting.

"How did she get here? Perhaps James is right after all."

The pony didn't look hurt. There was string tied like a bridle round her head and metal dangling from her mouth. Nicholas peered at her, and thought, "Oh gosh, a bicycle chain! What sort of people are these who can ride a pony with a bicycle chain in her mouth?" He felt a sense of fury mixed with a feeling of inadequacy. "How can I get her out?" he wondered, staring into the pit. And then he heard the sound of hoofs on the road outside, and he started to call, "Hullo. Nicholas here. Can you help? There's a pony in a pit. Come quickly," and Jubilee neighed again from the bottom of the pit.

"It's Nicholas," Maria exclaimed.

"And the pony must be Jubilee," James said.

"Leave your ponies outside. There are bottles very-where," called Nicholas.

"I know the pit. I came here once with some school-friends looking for scrap. There wasn't any. How did she get down here do you suppose?" James asked Maria.

"The same way as the others got to Hillsbridge."

"Hurry up!" called Nicholas. "Who are you, any-way?" He had hoped for Bromwyn. She was brainy, everybody knew that; and brains were more use than tidy clothes and an elegant hair-do on an occasion like this. "It sounds like Maria and James; that means I shall have to do the thinking. Put my thinking-cap on, as Ma says," decided Nicholas.

"I hope they don't get untied," said James, look-ing at the two ponies. "Come on."

The bank was slippery with rain, and already their clothes were clinging to their bodies. "They look like drowned rats," thought Nicholas. "It's Jubilee. She's been ridden. Look."

"With a bicycle chain," shouted Maria. "We can

"How can we get her out?"

have them up now for cruelty to animals. Poor Jubilee!"

James looked at the chestnut pony below him in the pit. She looked pitiful, and she was shivering.

"How can we get her out?" he asked.

"Exactly; how can we?" agreed Nicholas.

"I'll ride her up," shouted Maria. In a moment she was sliding down the side of the pit.

"Stop. Stop you idiot," shouted Nicholas.

But now she was sliding faster, falling, taking earth and stones with her, terrifying Jubilee.

"You're quite irresponsible," shouted Nicholas.

"You can't ride her up the sides. We need a winch, or a crane," James said. One of the ponies tied by the road neighed.

Maria was standing up now. Earth was plastered to her wet clothes. She started to pat Jubilee. Then she took the string off the pony's head and the chain out of her mouth. Jubilee was very nervous; every time Maria touched her she flinched. Her tail was tucked between her hind legs, her back was up; she looked half wild; so that Nicholas said, "She won't be the same pony when we get her back. She won't be any good for beginners, not ever again."

"We must do something. Audrey will be expecting Maria and me on Tango and Dawn soon. What are we going to do?" James asked. He was thinking, "Nicholas is wasting time. He's the eldest of us after all. He goes to an expensive school. His father was a captain in the army, surely Nicholas has a plan."

And Nicholas didn't know what to do.

"Maria had better stay here with Jubilee. I will go for help and you take the two ponies to the stables as fast as you can, James, and break the news. You must hurry, you understand?" he said.

"But will Maria be all right here?" asked James

doubtfully. "Supposing Jubilee gets excited when we leave?"

"We can't get her out anyway. Try to climb out, Maria," he said.

"I need a ladder. I'm not much good at climbing," replied Maria. Suddenly she was frightened and didn't want to be left alone in the pit with Jubilee; and all the time the rain kept falling on and on as though it would never stop. She was shivering now like the pony.

"You were a fool to go down there," cried Nicholas, angry because he was anxious and didn't know what to do.

"We're in a proper mess and no mistake," James said.

"But standing about won't help. For goodness' sake go to the stables, James. I will cope here," shouted Nicholas.

Because he was younger than Nicholas, James stifled his misgivings and hurried towards the road. The two ponies were still there. Behind them was a line of cars.

"So these are yours," shouted an angry motorist. "See what you've done. You've caused a three-mile queue."

All the cars seemed to be hooting at James and he was crimson now to his ears.

"There's a hurt pony in the wood," he shouted, vaulting on to Dawn.

"So what?" shouted an angry young man in a sports car. "Can't you see you've ruined our day by the sea? It was fine when we started; now look at it."

"I didn't make the weather," muttered James, riding the ponies along the verge. Behind him engines were revving up. Several people leaned out of car windows to shout caustic remarks. "I don't care," James told himself. "Let them shout. They don't know any better, poor things. They're townsmen . . ."

He always felt like a king when he was riding. No words could hurt him now. Presently the cars had gone and there was just the wet road ahead and the sea away on the left, sullenly beating against rocks. "Poor little Jubilee," thought James. "And what about Maria? Supposing she gets hurt in the pit? What a terrible day it's been."

"Are you sure you will be all right, Maria? I will come back with a ladder, I won't be long, I promise," said Nicholas who couldn't bear to stand another moment in the pouring rain staring down into the dismal pit.

Maria didn't mean Nicholas to know she was afraid. Her teeth were chattering. But soon Audrey would come in her battered car and after that everything would be all right because Audrey would know what to do.

"Yes, I'm all right thank you," she replied, and wondered what her two sisters were doing at the stables and if the eleven o'clock ride had gone out.

"Okay, if you're sure you're all right," Nicholas said, mounting Trombone. He was thinking, "I don't want to be blamed afterwards if anything awful happens."

He could hear cars revving their engines in the road. There seemed a lot of shouting. "Where am I going? What am I going to do?" he wondered desperately. "Find a farm I suppose. Farmers are always ready to help in an emergency."

Ivor and Stella were very wet. Ivor could imagine his mother's face when he returned home. "You'll be having double pneumonia next. You mark my words," she would say. His clothes would be snatched off him to dry in front of the old range. A hot drink would be pushed into his hand.

"I hope the horsebox will be here soon. What time is your bus, Stella?" he asked.

"I don't know really. I've missed the one I was supposed to catch. Mummy told me to do some shopping. I've got the list somewhere. Here it is. Wet, isn't it? *Bacon. Ham. Potatoes. Bananas. 1 lb. Fresh Haddock. Swiss Roll.* There won't be anything for tea. . . ." Stella pushed the sodden piece of paper back into her pocket. She was depressed now.

"I knew Patchwork would be hurt. I knew it in my bones right from the first. We've got to do something, Stella. You understand, don't you? We've got to watch the thugs."

"Yes, but how?"

"I bet James will think up something," Ivor said.

"I wish I lived near the riding-school," Stella said.

"Look, a horsebox," shouted Ivor. "Hurray. It's soon here, isn't it?"

"I don't know. I feel as though I've been here for hours."

"I'll race you to the gate. Come on, run."

But Stella wouldn't run. Her legs were stiff from standing. Ivor opened the gate, hurried to greet the horsebox driver while Stella stayed with her arm round piebald Patchwork.

"So these are the ponies. They don't look too good, do they? Do you think they can walk as far as the gate?"

The driver was a big burly man, with large arms. He wore an old shirt rolled up to the elbows, and a cap pulled half over his eyes.

"Come on, my dear," he said to Patchwork. The ponies were reluctant to move. "If it wasn't so wet I'd bring the box in; but with the ground as it is, we'd be bogged down inside ten minutes," the driver said.

"Do you know anything about teenage gangs on motor-bikes?" Ivor asked.

"There are plenty about. They make bikes too fast nowadays, that's the trouble."

The back ramp was down. Firecracker limped into the box; Patchwork followed. "That was easy, wasn't it?" the driver said. He didn't seem to notice the rain.

"Coming in front with me?" he asked.

"I think we had better travel with the ponies," Ivor answered.

"It's all the same to me."

The horsebox bumped and jolted out of the little yard.

"I wonder where Jubilee is," Stella said.

"I wonder."

They expected to pass James and Maria with Tango and Dawn. But presently they found themselves in a traffic jam. "We'll go another way," the driver called, and turned off the main road.

"There would be a jam today of all days," Stella said.

"Perhaps we'll see Nicholas," Ivor suggested.

They came to the stable-yard at last, as the sky was clearing. Daniel, Anne and Bromwyn greeted them.

"You'd better rush home and change. Gosh, you look wet," Anne said, taking the ponies as the horse-box rumbled away. "Audrey's taking out the eleven o'clock class. She's pretty glum as you can imagine. Poor old Patchwork."

"There isn't another bus until after lunch," Stella said.

"You'd better come to our place then, and get dry. Your mother will be furious if you catch a cold," Anne said.

"Mummy's never cross."

"Listen. Hoofs," said Bromwyn, "and in a hurry too. Whoever can it be?"

They pushed the two tired ponies into loose-boxes, and slammed the doors. "Surely it can't be James and Maria already," Anne said.

"Perhaps it's Nicholas returning with Jubilee," suggested Daniel, and Bromwyn thought that Daniel must be more intelligent than he looked, since he seemed to have learned their names already.

They ran into the road and now they could see James riding Dawn and leading Tango.

"Where's Maria?" thought Bromwyn. "What's happened? Why is he alone?" They all started to shout at once.

"Hullo. What's happened?"

"Where's Maria?"

"Have you seen Nicholas?"

"Is Maria hurt?"

James looked very wet. He had been trotting all the way from the wood, riding bareback, and all the time he had been worrying about Maria.

"Where's Audrey? More bad news. But Maria's all right. At least, I hope she is," he said, turning the ponies into the familiar stable-yard.

"Audrey's out. What's happened? We must know," shouted Bromwyn.

"All right, let me get off first. I've been trotting for miles bareback. Wait a minute. It's a long story," James said.

"I'm All Right, Thank You"

The ride was coming up the road now. The children waiting in the yard could see the slim figure of Audrey who was riding tall, dark brown Trooper. The class was following her. It was too small to make much of a clatter.

"There will be no free rides for weeks now," thought James. Everyone in the yard knew about Jubilee and Maria in the pit by this time. Anne stood nervously biting her nails. "What will Mummy say?" she wondered, for Mrs. Fisher was inclined to favour Maria, because she was the youngest, while Mr. Fisher would favour Bromwyn because she was the eldest.

The ride came into the yard. The children helped the riders off and took the ponies automatically as they always did.

"We can't tell her for a minute," Bromwyn said to the others. "Not until the pupils have gone."

Daniel stood about, not knowing what to do. He had big hands, Anne saw, was big altogether, with dark hair and a slightly hooked nose. She thought him ugly.

The pupils were gone at last.

"Well, let's look at Tango and Dawn now," Audrey said. "How did they come along, James?"

"All right. But there's a new disaster. Jubilee's in a pit. Maria's with her and Nicholas. I don't know how we'll ever get her out."

"She hasn't broken a leg or anything. You don't mean that, do you?" Audrey asked.

"No. But she's been ridden with a bicycle chain in her mouth. I came here as fast as I could. Audrey, there must have been some terrible people riding the ponies. We ought to go to the police. You ought to," James said. His clothes were drying on his body. He wondered how Jocelyn was getting on at home. Had the paying-guest arrived yet? Soon it would be lunchtime. He would have to go home soon; but how could he with Maria in the pit with Jubilee?

"There will be time to see the police later. I'll get a head-collar and lunge rein. We may be able to coax her out of the pit. Someone get some oats," Audrey said.

"I can't come I'm afraid, I have to go back to the hotel. I'll be back tomorrow," Daniel said, as though they should care or be sorry, which they weren't.

Daniel walked thoughtfully out of the yard. His parents would have spent the morning on the beach with his little sister Rosemary. He hoped they would do the same tomorrow; then perhaps he could bring a picnic lunch.

The sky had cleared. A rainbow stretched like coloured ribbon above the slag-heaps.

"Someone will have to stay behind and see to Patchwork and Firecracker and their wounds. Any volunteers?" asked Audrey. There was a choke in her voice now; and she seemed suddenly bent with fatigue.

"I've done a course in First Aid," Anne said.

"She came out top," Bromwyn added.

"I'll help you. You'll need someone to hold the ponies," said Stella.

"What about your bus?" asked someone.

"It doesn't matter."

"You should go home, James. You're soaked to the skin. And you, Ivor. I'll just take Bromwyn," Audrey said.

Nicholas came to a farm. There was a rainbow in the sky now. Everything was bright and sparkling after the rain. He found a man driving a tractor towards a field where stooks of corn were already drying in the sunlight.

He jumped a low stone wall and halted Trombone by the tractor. "I'm sorry to bother you," he began.

The man was reluctant to help at first. His eyes kept wandering towards the stooks of corn. His hands stayed on the steering-wheel and gears ready to move on. When Nicholas had finished explaining what had happened there was an uncomfortable silence. Nicholas wondered whether to offer money. Then he decided to play his last card, which was Maria; he hadn't mentioned her presence in the pit so far. Now he said, "You see there's a girl in the pit with the pony. I'm afraid if the pony gets excited, well, she'll be trampled on."

And the man turned the tractor without a word. Nicholas saw that he was small with rugged features and dark eyes.

"You know where the pit is?"

"I should do. It's mine as it happens," the man answered.

"I'll go on then." Nicholas jumped Trombone over the wall again; he couldn't help feeling a little triumphant. "James would never have got round that sullen chap on the tractor," he thought.

The road was still crammed with cars when he reached it. The wood looked more inviting now that the sun was shining. He couldn't hear the tractor coming yet. "Maybe the man's got to tell someone where he's going," Nicholas thought. He rode over the bank into the wood and a whinny came from the pit.

"Help's coming," Nicholas called. "Perhaps we'll get Jubilee out before Audrey arrives. There's a tractor coming."

Trombone whinnied to Jubilee. "Maria, are you there?" Nicholas called. He had a funny feeling in the pit of his stomach now. "Maria, Maria," he called. He came to the pit. Maria was crouching against the side.

"I'm all right; I just feel a bit sick, that's all," she said.

Jubilee was sweating and the ground in the pit was trampled and churned into mud.

"What happened?" asked Nicholas.

"Jubilee went a bit mad after you and Trombone left. I suppose she gave up hope or something. I couldn't do anything with her. She just seemed to go mad for a bit. I'm sorry. . . ."

"Why should you be sorry? Did she tread on you?" said Nicholas. He knew he was shouting because he was anxious. He didn't like the way Maria looked.

"Come on, what happened?" he shouted. He could hear the tractor coming along the road, and he started to wonder how it would get to the pit.

"She trod on me. It didn't hurt much. But now I feel funny . . ."

"What did she tread on? Did she hit your head?" shouted Nicholas.

"No, not my head. . . ."

Nicholas tied Trombone to a tree. "I shouldn't have gone for the tractor. I should have stayed, but how was I to know that? I only wanted to get help as quickly as possible. Anyone else would have done the same," he thought. Then he said to Maria:

"Now come on, speak up. Where are you hurt?" He shouted down into the pit.

"Shouting at the young lady won't help," said a quiet voice behind him, and he saw that the man on the tractor had arrived on the scene. He felt ashamed now, as he had once when his father had found him cutting up a live beetle with a pair of scissors.

"Is she badly hurt?" the man asked.

"I don't know," Nicholas said.

"I've got some ropes on the tractor. I'll try to back it up here." The man had a dog at his heels, Nicholas saw now; a wise hill sheepdog, the sort of dog which knows as much or more than his master.

"How are you feeling now?" asked Nicholas in his kindest voice, looking at Maria who was sitting up with her head in her hands.

"All right thank you . . ."

"She always says that; she's the sort of person who

always does out of habit," thought Nicholas. He could hear the tractor starting up. "I wish I had stayed at home," he thought. "I've been looking forward to this day for the whole of the summer term; what a day to look forward to!" The tractor was coming slowly towards him through the trees. "I'm going for a ladder," the man said, turning off the engine. Nicholas saw that he had lit a cigarette.

"How are you feeling now, Maria?" Nicholas asked again.

"All right, thank you. . . ."

But she didn't look all right.

"Your neck looks funny," Nicholas said.

"I've probably broken it."

"And you can die of a broken neck," Nicholas remembered.

"Don't move then, stay quite still. Do you hear?" She nodded and then cried, "Owh, owh . . ."

"Stay still. Don't move your head," shouted Nicholas.

Audrey knew where the wood was. Sitting beside her, Bromwyn wondered how Maria would be when they found her. Surely Nicholas wouldn't leave her. How deep was the pit, she wondered, and how on earth would they get Maria and Jubilee out?

"Are you going to do anything about all this?" she asked Audrey.

"In what way?"

"I mean catch the culprits."

"But we haven't a shred of evidence against anyone."

"What about the motor-bike tyre marks, and the piece of bicycle chain? Aren't they clues?" Bromwyn asked.

"My father once went to court over something. It cost him nearly five hundred pounds and he didn't get a penny back. We'll see if it happens again. If it does, then we'll act," Audrey said.

"By then there will hardly be a sound pony left," Bromwyn said, remembering how she had meant to paint; instead here she was in Audrey's battered car, speeding along a crowded road to find her sister and Jubilee.

Audrey drove as she rode – with the forward seat. It was as though she expected the car to lengthen its stride and jump at any moment.

"Here we are," she said, leaning back a little as she braked.

"It looks as though a tractor's been in the wood," Bromwyn said.

The day was hot now. The wood smelt of old forgotten food, of the tins rusting in the undergrowth. The ground was still wet from the rain and Bromwyn slipped climbing down the bank and pitched forward into the tins.

"Are you all right? Where's the pit? Do you know?" asked Audrey.

"Perhaps we'd better call. Nicholas, Nick. Maria," called Bromwyn and an answering shout came back.

"Sounds like Nicholas," said Bromwyn.

"I hope Maria isn't hurt. I shall feel horribly responsible if she is," Audrey said.

"But you didn't tell her to fall into the pit. Anyway James said she was okay. There's Trombone."

They started to run. "He's got help. Look, there's a tractor and a man," Bromwyn said. "Good old Nicholas." "Hullo," she called. "We're the relief squad. How goes it?"

"I don't know. This chap's helping. Here's the owner of the pony," he said turning to the man, who touched his cap before continuing to tie knots in a rope.

"We've got a ladder. Maria's not too good. I'm

afraid she may have broken her neck," Nicholas said.

"Oh no," shouted Audrey, while Bromwyn ran to the pit and, kneeling down on the edge, said, "Hullo, Maria. How are you?"

"I'm all right thank you . . ."

"That's all she says. How can you tell how bad she is when that's all she says?" grumbled Nicholas.

"We always get polite when we're ill; even Daddy does. . . ."

"I'm just going to put the ladder down. I don't think it's long enough, that's the trouble. It's only ten foot," the man said.

"Jubilee looks battered. Whoever has been mucking about with the ponies should go to Borstal or prison," exclaimed Bromwyn.

The man tied two lengths of rope to the ladder and slid it gently down the side of the pit. "It's hardly long enough. Perhaps we ought to get another one and lash them together."

"I'm all right, I can climb up it," Maria said.

"Oh no, not if you've got something broken you can't. I'll go back to the farm. I've got another ladder in the barn. Then we can carry you up; careful like. After that we'll see to the pony." The man returned to his tractor.

"Today is endless," thought Nicholas. "Did I really get up this morning and have breakfast at home?"

"What a wonderful man," said Audrey wearily.

"What do you think of Maria?" asked Bromwyn.

"It's difficult to say from up here. What happened, Nicholas?"

"I don't know. I wasn't here. I was fetching help from the farm. When I came back she was looking peculiar and all she says is, 'I'm all right thank you.' "

"Doesn't sound much like a broken neck to me. She ought to see a doctor though when we get her out," Audrey said.

Tied Up Like A Parcel

There was an invalid chair in the porch so James knew the paying-guest had arrived. He stopped to pat Dobbin, the big Shire horse he and the other children who helped at the riding-school had rescued a year ago. He didn't want to go home, didn't want to meet his tired mother, his sister who would ask a hundred questions, or the new paying-guest who would be certain to expect him to run errands for her.

Nothing seemed to alter the bungalow garden; it was always stony, and weeding the paths and drive only seemed to fetch up more stones. Still he could smell the sea; the air was sea air; and James loved the sea. He ran the last few steps to the bungalow, threw himself at the back door, charged into the kitchen as though he had been running the whole way home.... A joint of bacon was boiling on the gas cooker.

"Hullo, what news? What's happened? Miss Adams arrived early; so it was a good thing I gave up ... She's going to pay ten guineas a week to be here. Mummy says that means we'll be able to have regular riding lessons. Well, come on, what happened?" Jocelyn asked. The kitchen was misting up her spectacles – it was full of steam and the hot, rich smell of boiling bacon.

"Now take off your wet things at once, James. You should have been home ages ago. You're all skin and bone as it is. Here, I'll make you some cocoa. Now run along to your room and change, dear, and don't, I repeat *don't* make a noise," said Mrs. Allcott.

"Is the new P.G. nice?" James asked; but his mother only said, "Go and change. Hurry now!"

He changed and told Jocelyn what had happened.

"Audrey won't do anything. I know she won't; she's a defeatist by nature. I know it now . . . It'll be up to us to do something," he finished.

"I quite agree. I'll get my writing pad and jot down a few ideas. Wait a sec," Jocelyn said.

They couldn't sit in the front room, because it was now Miss Adams's domain.

Mrs. Allcott was dishing up the bacon in the kitchen.

"Let's try the garden. It's stopped raining," James said.

They found two deck-chairs and sat in them.

"How are we going to catch the culprits? That's the main point, isn't it?" asked Jocelyn.

"I don't know that the catching is so important. We need evidence; real cut-and-dried evidence," James said. Jocelyn wrote *EVIDENCE* in capital letters.

"It'll mean staying up all night," said James thoughtfully.

"We can't possibly fight people on motor-bikes," Jocelyn complained.

"I know. Wait a sec. I've got a plan."

"Mummy's calling. Come on, we'd better help. We should have laid the table," Jocelyn said, jumping to her feet.

"All right. But I know what we can do . . . It's the only thing we can do really. . . ." James answered, following his sister indoors. In his mind he saw a moonlit night, motor-bicycles carelessly parked among brambles, and he heard the gentle sound of ponies grazing, the creak of rusty hinges moving to open an old gate . . .

"That's right, James. You help too; there's no reason why Jocelyn should do everything," his mother said.

"What do we do now, Anne?" Stella asked.

They had bathed Firecracker's and Dawn's cut mouths and torn, swollen legs.

"Relax," Anne replied.

"It's obvious the ponies have been galloped along a road, isn't it, and through brambles and wire?" Stella said.

"Yes."

"Which means the fiends can ride a little."

"Yes and no; if you hold on by the reins, and are about fifteen you can stay on quite well for a bit," Anne said.

"Can you? It took me weeks to stay on at all," Stella answered.

"Riding motor-bikes may help you. I don't know, the whole business makes me feel pretty sick. How can people be so awful? What makes them like that?"

"I suppose they were showing off," suggested Stella.

"Yes, the boys to the girls; which means it was a mixed bunch of teenagers. To think that I'm a teenager too. . . ." said Anne.

"Telephone! Will you answer?"

Anne picked up the receiver.

"It's the Hotel Marina speaking . . . Can you take a little girl of six out this afternoon?" a voice asked.

"No, I'm afraid we're fully booked for the rest of the week," Anne said.

Putting down the receiver she wondered how Audrey would fare during the next few days. She would be losing money all the time, feeding lame ponies; and this was the time of year when she usually made up for the cold winter months, Anne recollected; for then the roads were slippery with ice, the fields as hard as rock, and no one came, while all the time the ponies continued eating as though they were each earning five pounds or more a week.

‘I’d better catch the next bus,” Stella said. “Mummy was expecting me early.”

She found her mackintosh. “I hope tomorrow is a nicer day,” she said.

“It can’t be much worse than today.”

“Can I ring you up and ask about Jubilee? I don’t want to bother Audrey,” Stella said.

“Of course, but ring up before eight.”

“Okay.”

It wasn’t far to the bus stop. Most of the way Stella could see the beach below. A crowd of holiday-makers waited for the bus. “I hope I get on,” thought Stella.

“Quick, I want my dinner, Mum,” cried Ivor. “Dreadful things have been happening. You wouldn’t believe your ears. We’re in for a battle, if you ask me; a real battle . . .”

“Whatever do you mean? And what’s this shouting for your dinner, who do you think you are? You’re soaked anyway. You’ll be having double pneumonia next, that you will,” said Mrs. Jones.

Ivor told his story, undressing at the same time.

“Now don’t you start scrapping with that bad lot on motor-bikes, do you hear, Ivor? I won’t have it,” his mother said, opening the oven door. “Your sister’s boyfriend rides a motor-bike, after all.”

“I can’t help that. We’ve got to do something. Otherwise Audrey will be out of business and what will I do then? You’ll have me hanging round your neck all the time. Not too much stew please, I must get back in a moment. I want to see if they’ve got Jubilee back yet.”

He burnt his mouth wolfing down the stew. Afterwards there was rice pudding out of a tin. Then he was running back along the street between the terrace houses, taking a short cut across a rubbish dump . . .

Ivor ran back, taking a short cut across a rubbish dump

miners were coming home from the first shift in the pits so he knew it was past two o'clock. His father would be home soon, washing in the kitchen, unless he had had a bath at the pit, as he sometimes did. He would eat the rest of the stew; afterwards, reading the paper, he would rest his tired feet on the kitchen table.

Anne was by herself in the stable-yard when Ivor reached it. "Any news?" he asked.

"No, nothing. I've given the ponies their lunch. I think I ought to go home. Can you take over?"

"That's all right, I'll manage. Don't you worry yourself, Anne," Ivor answered, looking at her anxious face.

"I can't help wondering about Maria. They've been such a long time. But I must go home, because Mummy was expecting me back for lunch. I was going to help her in the garden."

Watching Anne go Ivor felt anxious too. He had always liked Maria. "She shouldn't have gone down into the pit," he thought; "but then that's Maria all over. She never will count the cost. She's impulsive. Doesn't think. . . ."

He visited each of the ponies and filled up one or two water buckets. The yard seemed horribly quiet; almost as though it was waiting for fresh tragedy. He found a dandy brush and groomed Northwind, though he was hardly dirty. Then he started to clean tack. He began to wish that something would happen; that at least the telephone would ring. The hurt ponies were depressingly quiet, resting their battered legs and not eating the hay hanging by their noses in haynets.

There wasn't a lot of tack to clean; when it was done, Ivor started to polish the buckles on head-collars. "Anything's better than sitting and thinking," he decided. "But soon we'll have to get down to working something out. James will have a plan, he always does;

he's better at plans than Nicholas though you wouldn't think it by looking at him," Ivor decided.

The ladders were lashed together now. "I'll fetch the girl up," said the man from the farm, and no one argued.

"I can climb up. I'm all right, thank you," Maria said when he reached the bottom of the pit.

But the man spoke to her as he did to animals. "Now don't you worry. I'll get you out all right... You'll see," he said in a soothing voice.

"Mind her neck," shouted Nicholas.

"I can't look. Supposing her neck is broken. Moving her could kill her. Oh dear, oh dear, oh dear," cried Bromwyn turning away from the pit.

"And they would all blame me," thought Nicholas. "But she can't be too bad. She keeps talking, doesn't she?"

"Don't jolt her," Audrey shouted.

"I can't perform a miracle. I can't bring her up without moving her at all," the man called from the bottom of the pit.

"I'm frightened," muttered Bromwyn.

"For goodness' sake stop panicking. It doesn't help anyone," Nicholas said.

The man was coming up the ladder with Maria over his shoulder. He had tied a scarf round her neck to give it support. Maria was smiling.

"I can't see why we're all fussing. She looks all right," Nicholas said, and a great wave of relief engulfed him.

"Maria, are you really all right?" Bromwyn asked.

"Yes, thank you. . . ."

They were up now. "You see I can stand," Maria said. "My legs feel a bit wobbly and my neck a bit stiff, that's all."

"You ought to have an X-ray," Audrey said. "And that means hospital."

"I'm all right," argued Maria.

"But we must be sure," Audrey answered.

"What about the pony? Can someone help me fix her in a rope sling?" the man asked.

"Yes, I will," offered Nicholas.

"You'd better let me. She knows me so well," said Audrey.

"I've got to tie a few more knots in the rope. I'm making a sort of net to go round her belly; then the tractor will pull her up if we can get it near enough," the man said.

"I don't know what we would have done without you," replied Audrey.

"For goodness' sake sit down, Maria. What happened? Why don't you say? Are you concussed or something?" asked Bromwyn.

"Right. Now we'll go down. I expect you know how to throw a pony all right."

"I don't know about that," Audrey said.

"This seems the longest day of my life," Nicholas muttered.

"I wish we could go now. I'm sure Maria should be in bed," Bromwyn said.

"We've got to see it out to the bitter end," Nicholas answered.

There was a thud as Jubilee fell.

"That man is a genius. Honestly Nicholas, how did you find him?" Bromwyn asked.

"Poor little Jubilee's all tied up like a parcel now," Maria said.

"I can't see how she got down there in the first place," Nicholas replied.

"Do stop looking down, Maria," shouted Bromwyn.

The man came up, tied the long ropes to the tractor. "All right, Miss Lewis?" he called. "Righty ho . . ."

He drove the tractor forward, shortened the ropes.

"All set," he called, reversing the tractor.

"Keep away from the side of the pit," Nicholas said to the girls.

"We're not imbeciles," Bromwyn replied, looking at her sister, trying to gauge how much she was hurt, if at all.

The tractor strained; the ropes creaked. "Supposing they break?" wondered Bromwyn.

Audrey was coming up the ladder now.

"Gently does it," the man said, and now the children could see a pair of grey ears.

"Hurray," shouted Bromwyn.

"Thank goodness it's nearly over," thought Nicholas. "I'm going straight home after this. I've had enough for one day."

Jubilee was lying on the ground now. Audrey and the man started to untie the ropes. "I don't know how to thank you enough," she said.

"That's all right," the man said.

When the last knot was untied Jubilee leapt to her feet and shook herself violently.

"I'd better take Maria to hospital now. Who can take Jubilee home?" Audrey asked.

"I will," Bromwyn answered.

"I would rather you came with me," Audrey said.

"And that leaves me; me the obvious choice; and I meant to go home," Nicholas thought. He couldn't help remembering lunch, no doubt still waiting for him in the simmering oven of the Aga in the Manse.

"I'll lead her, I can ride Trombone," he said.

"Oh, thank you. You are an angel. You've all been marvellous," Audrey said, and she started to thank the man all over again.

Nicholas mounted Trombone. "What shall I do with Jubilee when I get back to the stables?" he asked.

"You'll have to tie her up. All the boxes are occupied. Can you walk as far as my car, Maria, do you think?" asked Audrey.

A bird flew out of the undergrowth. Flies hovered round Jubilee's torn mouth.

"I'm all right, thank you," said Maria, walking slowly towards Audrey's car.

"Come on, Jubilee. Trombone, stop squealing. Come on, both of you," shouted Nicholas.

"I'll lead Jubilee over the bank for you if you like," offered Bromwyn.

The rainbow had gone from the sky. Somehow one knew that late afternoon had come.

"Come on, Bromwyn," called Audrey, starting the car.

"See you later, Nick," Bromwyn said, handing him Jubilee's reins.

"I must get home before dark," Audrey said in desperate tones. "Probably I shall have to have the vet again for more anti-tetanus injections. . . ."

"I hate hospitals," Maria said. "I'm quite all right so why can't I go home?"

"I wish we were on the telephone at home," Bromwyn said.

"We're nearly there. It's a nice little hospital. I've been X-rayed there lots of times," Audrey told them.

A Cracked Neck

"You have cracked a vertebra. You are lucky that it isn't worse," the doctor said, looking at the X-ray.

"Oh no! Oh dear! What does that mean?" asked Bromwyn.

"Rest; and I think we'll put it in plaster just to be safe."

The doctor started to write. The last of the evening sun filtered gold and red through the frosted window-panes.

"Will you wait outside again please. . . ."

"How well we know this corridor," Bromwyn said to her sister as they sat down on the chairs near the small food-bar which was shut.

"This is the third time we've waited here, isn't it?" Maria asked.

"Yes. They are going to send us home by ambulance which means one last wait after you've seen the plasterer. Audrey arranged that before she left, while you were in the X-ray room. She couldn't wait any longer. She said she would tell Mummy what had happened. She was very upset really. . . ."

"That will be the fourth time," Maria said. "What is the time anyway?"

"Nearly half-past eight."

"I shan't be able to ride again for weeks, will I?"

"No. Not till your neck has been X-rayed again. You can't even run till then, or lift heavy things," Bromwyn answered.

"It would happen in the holidays. What are we going to do about the beasts on motor-bikes? Not that I shall be able to help. Oh, how I hate sitting still. I shall have to knit or something."

"The plasterer has arrived. Look, he's beckoning. We'll soon be home now," Bromwyn said.

When Maria's neck was in plaster the two girls waited again in the corridor by the food-counter (which was still closed) for an ambulance. Casualties were still coming in; mostly teenagers who had crashed on motor-bikes.

"It's always like this on Saturdays. We get the motor-bike casualties and, in the winter, the football ones as well," a nurse said.

Finally there was a vacant ambulance.

"Gosh, I'm tired," Bromwyn said. "Too tired for plans, too tired for anything."

"Supposing the gang strikes again tonight?" asked Maria, while the driver of the ambulance wrapped a rug round her knees.

"We can't do anything now. Tomorrow we'll make a plan," Bromwyn said.

Mrs. Fisher met them in the road outside the cottage.

"We thought you were never coming. Have you had anything to eat? Can you walk up the path?" she asked.

"I'm all right, thank you. It's only cracked. . . ."

"I've put the soup on," Anne called from the cottage.

They clambered through scaffolding. Maria was suddenly too weary for words; her neck started to ache.

"Everything's such a muddle – the house, the ponies, everyone," she shouted and burst into tears.

The yard was silent when Audrey returned to it, except for the steady sound of teeth munching hay. Then, from a tree, a guinea fowl seeing the lights of her car started to squawk; and the dogs began to yap in the cottage. She could hear the telephone ringing in the saddle-room. "Maria's broken her neck by the sound of things; there's hardly a pony left fit to work, and the holidays are just beginning," she thought wearily. "I can't go on much longer. I really can't."

She picked up the telephone receiver.

"Your ponies are out," a voice said. "I thought you ought to know. . . ."

"Who is it speaking?" she asked. "Who is it?" But the voice had rung off. She rang the exchange. "Please trace that last call. Where did it come from?" she asked.

"From a call-box."

"Thank you." She put down the receiver. "The ponies are at home," she thought. "All of them. Why are people doing this to me? Perhaps there is really a gang on motor-bikes." The dogs welcomed her when she went inside the cottage and there was a notice propped against the kettle which read: *All animals fed, Ivor.*

"Come on, dogs," she said and went back to the yard to turn out some of the ponies into the paddock behind the stables. There was a moon now; and the flash of headlights passing along the road, and the lights of ships out at sea.

She went back to the telephone, and found the diary. "Who shall I put off for tomorrow?" she wondered. "When will the lame ponies be sound again? I'll ring the Grand Hotel first," she decided. "Hullo. Can I speak to Mrs. Thurston? Yes. It's the riding-school here . . ." she began.

"And now we must decide what to do," James said the next morning, sitting in the granary biting a piece of straw.

"That's what we're here for, isn't it?" asked Nicholas, who had ridden over on his bicycle.

"Anne's backed out. She says she wants to help Mummy, and Maria's out of course," Bromwyn said.

"We ought to keep watch, that's what we ought to do," Ivor suggested.

"What, every night?" Jocelyn asked.

"Not all night. Till midnight."

"They may never come again," Nicholas said.

"It's the only thing we can do," James answered.

"We'll have to get Audrey to put the ponies back in the bottom meadow then," Jocelyn said.

Ivor could imagine himself now waiting by the gate behind the brambles in the darkness of a summer night. He could hear the motor-bikes coming towards him down the lane; the ponies in the field behind him cropping the grass.

"There will have to be three of us waiting for them. Someone will have to go for the police," he said.

"Naturally," agreed Nicholas.

"All we want is evidence," James said.

"But we haven't got any," Bromwyn said.

"Next Friday and Saturday nights should be the nights," Ivor said. "That's the nights the motor-bikes go roaring down our street."

"We must speak to Audrey then," Stella said, and suddenly the granary was tense with excitement and they all knew at once how they would feel, waiting for the motor-bikes in the gathering darkness.

"How many do you think there will be?" asked Bromwyn.

"About six or seven I should think," answered James.

"They may not come at all," Nicholas said.

"They will, if I know anything about them," Ivor answered.

"Isn't this place miserable now? I mean the riding-school. Audrey walks about like someone in a nightmare. Have you noticed?" Stella asked.

"The ponies look better today anyway. Patchwork's the worst. Jubilee's quite sound," Bromwyn answered.

"Will Constable Wilson come if we ask him to, do you think?" Stella asked.

"You mean if we see the motor-bikes?" asked Bromwyn.

"I think we should ring the station in the town as well – there's generally a patrol car about at night," James said.

"If only Audrey would co-operate. . . ."

"Mummy's not going to like it," James said.

"Nor is my mother. I hadn't thought of that," Stella muttered.

And now they were all thinking of their parents.

"If only Maria hadn't hurt herself. It was all so unnecessary really," Bromwyn grumbled.

"Completely," agreed Nicholas. "I don't think Ma will mind me staying out late. I mean I'm not a little boy any more." He was always conscious of being the eldest among the helpers at the riding-school, though Bromwyn was only a few months younger. Sometimes they all seemed absurdly childish to him; at other times they seemed almost his contemporaries.

Bromwyn smiled at him now. "Mummy wouldn't mind too much normally; as long as she knew where I was and with whom but Maria's neck has shaken her."

"I can just slip out when everyone's in bed. Dad turns in early because of going out for the early shift; and my sister, well, she never notices where I am," Ivor said.

"Then all we have to do is to get round our parents and persuade Audrey to put the ponies in the bottom meadow," James said. He had to go home now. "Come on, Jocelyn. It's nearly eleven o'clock," he said.

"We've got to take a registered parcel to the post office for Miss Adams," Jocelyn explained. "We'll be over tomorrow."

"And I'm going out to tea," Stella said to no one in particular.

They started to leave the granary. Ivor had brought sandwiches. It was very hot now; the first really hot day of the summer. Flies were everywhere, and there was the heady smell of the sea. The sun showed up the dirty windowpanes of the loose-boxes.

"Next holidays let's paint the stables for Audrey," Ivor suggested.

"Too much work," said Nicholas idly, mounting his

bicycle. "What about coming to tea tomorrow, Bromwyn?"

"When do we meet again – Friday morning?" asked James. "I'm going to swim this afternoon," he thought. "Swim and dream and watch out for motor-bikes. I might pick up a clue on the beach; one never knows."

"Yes, Friday about eleven. I've given up getting up early," Nicholas said.

"I'll ask Mummy about tea tomorrow," Bromwyn said.

"It's a long time to Friday," grumbled Ivor. "Who's going to ask Audrey about putting the ponies in the bottom meadow?"

"You can if you like," called Nicholas over his shoulder, pedalling away down the road, thinking, "I'll ride this evening when it's cool and the flies have gone; the beach will be empty then."

"Audrey, will you put the ponies in the bottom meadow on Friday and Saturday night please? We want to keep watch then," Ivor said.

"I may need to before then. I can't keep feeding hay to them. It's too expensive," Audrey answered.

"Then we'll keep watch earlier."

"I'm going to put wire above the gate and a padlock on the chain. . . ."

"What about nails for the motor-bike tyres?" suggested Ivor.

"Might go into the ponies' hoofs instead."

"Why do you think people are doing this to the ponies?" Ivor asked; and for the first time he wondered whether the gang might somehow be connected with Jim Morgan – who the children had helped to catch smuggling a year ago.

He felt frightened then. "Supposing they're full grown men on motor-bikes?" he wondered.

"I don't know. But it's happened before. A gang

killed a pony in the north of England a little time back," Audrey said.

"My sister's boyfriend rides a motor-bike," Ivor said.

"I'm sure he's got nothing to do with it. Stop worrying, Ivor," Audrey answered.

"Where's the parcel? Yes, I'll bring back the receipt. Anything else, Miss Adams?" James asked.

"No, my dear; nothing more this morning."

James was glad that he wasn't old, with two sticks, a wavering voice and thin, wrinkled hands. "I won't be long, and I'll bring back the receipt," he promised again.

"That's right, my dear."

More than anything James wanted to swim now. He could see people splashing in the sea. Daniel was in the post office buying stamps with his sister Rosemary.

"How's Maria?" he asked.

"Suffering from a broken neck," James answered. He was impatient now for Friday night; to follow the track to the field in the gathering dusk. "I wish we were going to watch tonight," he thought. "There's too much waiting in life. Perhaps we'll have to fight, who knows?" He waved good-bye to Daniel, ran home along the road beneath the sweltering sun. All the time in his imagination he was living Friday night, could smell the smoky, sooty smell of the goods trains, going along the line beyond the bottom meadow, lighting up the dark slag-heaps beyond as night came.

"Thank you, dear. Here's sixpence for your trouble," said Miss Adams taking the receipt. "I'll share it with Jocelyn – threepence each," James thought, and he stood for a second imagining burly figures in crash helmets standing in bright summer moonlight.

"You *are* a daydreamer, dear," Miss Adams said.

"Can I go out on Friday evening? It's frightfully important," Stella asked her mother as they ate their tea, in the flat where they lived high above the holiday-makers and buses below in the street.

"How late? Where to? You know I'm not difficult, and I don't want to be tiresome, darling, but one has to draw the line somewhere," her mother said. Stella knew suddenly how difficult it was going to be for her to join the others by the bottom meadow on Friday night.

"I could stay with someone. With Bromwyn for instance; she's quite old, and sensible too," Stella said.

"She's the sister of the girl who broke her neck, isn't she?"

"That's right."

"But why do you want to stay out late? Is there a bonfire party or something?"

"Not exactly. But there will be a lot of us. Nicholas too; he's nearly grown up. . . . ."

"Does Miss Lewis know about it? I suppose you're out to catch the gang on motor-bikes. Is that it?"

"Yes. Please let me go, Mummy. Everyone else is going. We're not going to fight or anything. We only want to fetch the police."

"Well, ask me again nearer the day. I'm too tired to decide anything now."

"All right." Stella was sure now that she could go. "Nothing can happen to us. People don't attack children. We'll be all right. It's going to be terrific fun. I'll take a torch and something to eat," she thought.

"I wish I had a bicycle," she said suddenly. "Can I have one for my birthday? A second-hand one will do."

In the end Nicholas schooled Trombone. He wanted to enter her in the local riding-club's Novice Dressage Test in September; and later in One-day Events. He marked himself out an arena with stones and decided that tomorrow he would ask Bromwyn to paint the appropriate letters for him. "I'll borrow a tennis marker from someone, and mark the centre with an X," he decided, practising a turn on the forehand. "Perhaps Bromwyn will judge me tomorrow. It doesn't need an expert to decide whether you are halting straight or not."

The future started to look hopeful as he rode. He stopped worrying about Audrey's plight, and could only see his own future ahead; himself a potential competitor at Badminton, even selected for training as a possible for a British Olympic team.

"Dinner," called his mother. "Nick, dinner." He halted his mare on the bit, her hocks under her. He saluted an imaginary judge and turned towards the house. Twilight had come and with it the sound of a summer's evening.

"You might mow the lawn tomorrow evening, Nicholas," his father said at dinner; and the days ahead of Nicholas seemed to stretch bright and hopeful, lit by the glowing lamp of success.

"That's all right, Pa. I'll do it in the morning. Bromwyn's coming to tea, I hope," he said.

He started to eat biscuits and cheese. "I don't suppose the gang on motor-bikes will ever turn up again. Friday evening is really going to be rather a bore," he decided. "But if I don't go, they will think I'm afraid to go, or some other bosh, and well, if it comes to a fight I'm not too bad with my fists." Above all Nicholas had a good opinion of himself, most of the time at any rate.

He dried up the dinner things for his mother, and then lay on his bed listening to the wireless in his small, crowded bedroom. "Tomorrow Bromwyn will be here," he thought. "I wish she would paint a picture for me; one of Trombone preferably."

Maria was cross. "It's so dull," she kept saying, over and over again.

Anne was helping her mother to make plum jam.

"I can go to tea with Nicholas tomorrow, can't I, Mummy?" asked Bromwyn, coming in with the dust of the stable-yard still on her shoes.

"I don't know. I don't know whether I trust that boy any more. He didn't look after Maria very well, did he?" Mrs. Fisher said, testing the boiling jam on a saucer for the third time.

"Maria didn't have to rush into the pit," Bromwyn answered.

The workmen had gone. The girls' sitting-room was nearly complete.

"We're going to buy curtain material tomorrow afternoon. Don't you want to come?" asked Mrs. Fisher.

"No, thank you. I might be able to ride Trombone; one never knows with Nick."

Bromwyn kept walking up and down thinking of Friday night. Supposing they caught the culprits, what then? Supposing they raced off on their infernal motor-bikes. Would it be enough to take their numbers?

"I want to go out on Friday night too please. It's all in order, we're all going," she said.

"All?" asked her mother.

"Stella, James, Jocelyn, Ivor, me, Nick."

"And me," added Anne.

Mrs. Fisher turned to switch on the kitchen light. "Maria can't go, that's definite," she replied.

Ivor ate his tea and went to bed. He didn't mean to ask about Friday night, not at all. It would come soon enough, he reckoned, and afterwards life would seem very tame. But in a year or two he would be off to be a stable-lad and after that there would be the racecourse and the cheering crowds, and one day his horse would be led in a winner. The street outside was quiet tonight, though he could hear a baby crying in the house next door.

"Poor Maria, she's going to miss all the fun," thought Ivor, before he fell asleep to dream of making his bed in a racing-stable, where the sheets kept turning into straw, but by the time he fetched a pitchfork, they were always sheets again.

A Waste of Time

Friday came wet and dismal.

"It would rain today," Stella said kissing her mother good-bye.

She had packed a bag with pyjamas and a change of clothes. The flat always seemed very empty when her mother had gone to work. Stella shook the table-cloth out of the window before she locked the door behind her and ran down the two flights of stairs into the impressive hall below.

Outside the street was shining wet and the buses splashed in the gutters; shoppers hurried by, stooping slightly beneath the rain; dispirited holiday-makers waited to catch the same bus as Stella.

"Today has arrived," thought Stella. "I hope we catch them. They deserve to go to prison; but I expect they'll be put on probation unless they're criminals already."

"Three cancellations, would you like a ride, Stella?" asked Audrey when Stella reached the stables.

Only Patchwork was still lame, though Firecracker was still resting and the ponies with sore mouths were being ridden in rubber snaffles.

"Yes please," Stella said.

Ivor arrived next, clutching a parcel.

"Just a few weapons," he explained mysteriously.

"There's to be no fighting," Audrey said. "Here's Tango's tack; put it on please, Stella."

"They won't come if it rains, will they?" Ivor asked, watching Stella bridling Tango.

"I don't suppose so. I'm staying the night with the Fishers."

"I wish I knew more about motor-bikes. Would sugar in the petrol-tanks stop them working?" Ivor asked.

"Search me."

"We must decide more," Ivor said, starting to throw stones at the paddock gate.

"Stop it," shouted Audrey. "We don't have people here who throw stones."

"I'm riding this morning," Stella said.

"I wish *I* was. I'm going to creep out tonight. I haven't asked Mum or Dad; I was too afraid they would say no. They do sometimes," Ivor said.

"But supposing they catch me," he wondered. "If I slip on the stairs. Oh well, I can still ask can't I?"

"Good-bye all. I'll be back this evening with Stella," Bromwyn said, pushing a packet of sandwiches into her jeans pocket.

"She'll have to have one of the bunks in your room. If she's going with you tonight, you'll have to look after her," Mrs. Fisher replied.

The alterations to the kitchen were nearly complete. "All we need now is a stable and a horse inside. Something of about fifteen hands, preferably a dark brown mare," Bromwyn thought. "We could do with a paddock, too, if it comes to that. If only one's dreams would come true. Tonight will be fun though. I love being out at night. But if it's still raining we'll have to call the whole thing off."

Far below the beach was deserted; the waves grey, sullenly beating the sodden sand; the sea empty, the clouds low, moving swiftly across the sky.

Then Bromwyn saw a piece of blue sky and she thought, "It's large enough to make a sailor a pair of trousers, and that means that it's going to be fine." She started to sing *Jingle bells, jingle bells, jingle all the way*, though it wasn't very appropriate for the time of year.

"And in the evening we'll wait at the end of the track. I'll take a thermos of coffee, the big one; and some chocolate. We'll have to plan everything very carefully. Nick will take charge, I expect; he generally does. I hope Daniel doesn't want to come. I'm sure he's hopeless in an emergency. He's a town person really; it's written all over him; even when he touches a horse you know it. I expect he lives in London. His parents must be very rich if they can stay at the Grand Hotel, rich but without much taste. Daddy says the hotel is a monument to ugliness."

She had reached the stables now, and it was still raining.

"Hullo. I've brought a suitcase. Can I really stay with you tonight?" called Stella.

"We're late. Come on, run, Jocelyn," shouted James hanging up the tea-towel. "Hurry!"

He knew now that he wouldn't be able to wait for anything, that all day he would be in a tearing hurry, simply because he was excited about the evening. He couldn't bear to sit down. Twice his mother had said, "James dear, you're like a cat on hot bricks."

Before breakfast he had been to see Dobbin, the grey Shire horse. The day had been fine then, and he had stopped to pull up ragwort growing in the Morgans' field. It had been a very quiet morning and for a moment he had felt at peace; then he had thought of the evening, had imagined the motor-bikes roaring along the road, and his blood had started to race in his veins. He had run back to the bungalow to drag his sister from her bed, crying, "Come on, Jocelyn. It's to-day. Wake up."

His mother had followed him saying, "James, be quiet! James, what are you thinking of, you'll wake up Miss Adams, James, James."

He had gone to wash, running the taps furiously in the bathroom, cleaning his teeth with frantic haste. The rain had started outside and he could see the evening ruined.

"Has anyone heard the forecast?" he cried, running into the kitchen. Of course, nobody had. His father had just finished breakfast; his mother was emptying the teapot; the rain was coming down in torrents outside.

"You're too late," his father said.

Now it was ten to ten. He had been to the post office for Miss Adams, and had fed the chickens they had now in an ark hen-house and run on the back lawn.

"We're late," he said slamming the back door.

"But what's the hurry? Sometimes I think you're mad, James," Jocelyn said.

She couldn't keep up with him. The rain beat against her spectacles. Her legs started to ache. "I'm not going to wait," he shouted, and ran on, his head bowed against the rain.

When he reached the yard the ten o'clock ride had gone out and Stella was riding the spare pony which one of the Allcotts might have been offered had they been earlier.

"Hullo, you are late," Bromwyn said. "But then, nearly everyone is late this morning. Where's Nicholas for instance?"

"Who wants to come early on such a miserable morning?" asked James.

The rain beat against Jocelyn's spectacles

"And what about tonight?" asked Jocelyn.

"There was enough blue to make a sailor's trousers," Bromwyn replied.

"And I'm staying with the Fishers whatever happens," Stella said.

The gutters on the loose-boxes were overflowing. A few bedraggled strands of straw lay outside the hay-shed.

Stella started to shiver.

"It must clear up by this evening. It's got to," James said.

During the afternoon there was a thunderstorm; then, as evening came, the sky lightened. The stable-yard seemed suddenly full of hope. Three ponies were turned out in the bottom meadow.

"I'll be back at eight," said Nicholas, disappearing on his bike.

James and Jocelyn were at home again by this time, staring out of the kitchen window at the changing sky.

"It's going to be all right," James said.

"We'd better take macs all the same," replied prudent Jocelyn.

"They make a noise; they rustle, mine does anyway."

"You know what Mummy said?"

"What?"

"If we were silly and irresponsible tonight, she would never let us stay out after bedtime again."

"We had better take our macs then," James answered.

They sat down to tea; to scrambled eggs on toast, bread, butter, jam, cake and biscuits.

"You're not to stay out after nine o'clock, is that clear?" asked Mr. Allcott. "And you're to come straight back."

"Yes," Jocelyn replied.

"And there's to be no fighting. I don't want your names in the paper. Once is enough," he continued.

"We're not meeting the others till ten to eight; and it's only ten to six now," James complained.

Because of Miss Adams they were having tea in the kitchen. "Do eat some more, James. You know what the doctor said," exclaimed Mrs. Allcott as James prepared to leave the table.

"I've had two slices of bread and the scrambled eggs," he answered.

He couldn't help looking at the clock every other minute.

"Let's go now," he said to Jocelyn when the tea was cleared away.

"It's awfully early."

"It doesn't matter."

They put on their mackintoshes and Jocelyn found a torch. Their parents said things like, "Don't be late," and "Don't get run over," and "Come straight home."

The road was still wet with rain, but over the sea the sky was red, promising a fine tomorrow.

"I feel quite sick with excitement," James said.

"We've missed the pops," complained Jocelyn.

"You can always go back and follow later," James said.

"No thank you."

He started to whistle and his hands went deep into the pockets of his mackintosh. "Oh, it's exciting isn't it!" he exclaimed suddenly, and now they were round the last bend passing the notice which read, *THE SEASHORE SCHOOL OF EQUITATION*, so that you expected the yard to be rather grand instead of only seven loose-boxes, a granary, a tiny cottage and a few sheds.

James couldn't help running a few steps now, though when they reached the yard it was deserted except for the horses munching hay in the loose-boxes.

"We are too early," Jocelyn said.

"Better early than late," James replied, starting to pace the yard. "We need a plan," he said, once stopping to look beyond the yard to the railway-line.

"You're sleeping in my room, Stella," Bromwyn said, putting the battered blue suitcase on her bed. "You don't mind, do you?"

"Lucky things! Oh, I do envy you. Why is life so mean to me?" cried Maria.

"I'm coming too," Anne said.

The three Fisher girls all in one room were a little overwhelming. "I'm sure I shall sleep beautifully," Stella said.

"Wow, the pops!" cried Maria. "We've missed five minutes already."

They all clattered down the narrow cottage stairs, so that Mr. Fisher called, "Quietly. On your toes. You sound like a herd of elephants."

Stella was frightened of Mr. Fisher with his wild, untidy hair, his paint-stained hands and his ability to say extraordinary things. Her mouth would go dry when she met him, sentences would rise in her throat to be spoken, only to be rejected a second later as unsuitable.

"We're going to hear the pops, Daddy," retorted Maria, "We're late already."

Later Bromwyn, Anne and Stella set off for the stables armed with a thermos of coffee, two torches and some string.

"One always needs string," Anne said. "At least that's my experience."

"I've got some pennies, in case we need to telephone." Stella said a moment later.

"Oh, well done!" Bromwyn answered.

"Well, it was Mummy's idea actually."

People were still on the beach; the sun was setting above the sea.

"Red night, shepherd's delight," quoted Bromwyn.

James and Jocelyn were looking rather forlorn sitting on upturned buckets when they reached the yard.

"At last. We thought no one was ever coming," called James.

"We had to listen to the pops," Anne said.

"It's only half-past seven," said Bromwyn.

"That means only another twenty minutes."

"We seem to have been here hours and hours already," complained James.

"Well, if you must be early," replied Bromwyn, "you must expect to wait."

"Why are you gulping your food, Ivor? You'll have stomach-ache, really you will," said Mrs. Jones.

"What's the hurry, son?"

"There isn't any hurry."

Ivor kept wondering why it was necessary to be at the stable-yard by ten to eight; it had upset all his plans. He would have to leave with his parents' permission.

"I want to meet a few friends," he said, helping himself to cheese. "Do you mind, Mum?"

"What friends?"

"The ones at the riding-school."

"But you've been with them all day. Why don't you live at Miss Lewis's, that's what I wonder sometimes," his father said.

The television was on. His father liked the children's programmes, more than Ivor sometimes.

"Bye Mum, 'bye Dad," Ivor said. "See you later."

"And mind it isn't too late," his father called after him.

The road was quiet at last; everything looked washed and sparkling after the rain.

Ivor started to run. He hadn't a mackintosh, just his everyday shorts, a thick jersey and plimsolls so that he could creep. "Shouldn't be more than six lads on the motor-bikes," he decided, turning into the stable-yard.

"The whole thing's rather a waste of time," thought Nicholas mounting his bicycle for the fourth time that day. "Probably the chaps on motor-bikes are miles away by now, and I wanted to watch the film on television tonight."

He called to Trombone as he pedalled along the drive and she lifted her head and looked at him. He wore a thick shirt with a scarf tucked into the neck, corduroy trousers, a cap pulled low over one eye. He had a cigarette and matches in one pocket, money and a knife in another. "I shan't stay long," he decided. "If they *are* coming they'll come before nine . . . We won't fight them away, though I'd like to have a go at them," he thought, bracing his fists so that his bicycle began to wobble.

"Here's Nicholas," cried James when he reached the yard.

"At last," exclaimed Ivor.

"Hullo Nick," called Bromwyn.

"Am I late then?"

"Well, it's eight o'clock," replied James, looking at the clock in the saddle-room.

"What's the plan?" Nicholas asked.

"That half of us should hide by the field, the others, the girls I suppose, at the top of the lane so that they can go for the police when the motor-bikes arrive," James said. His face was pale now. He kept biting his nails, kicking stones around the yard, picking things up only to put them down a second later, anything but stay still.

"But how are we to know they mean to hurt the

ponies? Supposing we fetch the police and they are simply picnicking? We'll look fools then, won't we?" asked Nicholas who hated to look a fool.

"Does that matter so much?" asked James.

"But surely we'll know somehow. They'll carry string, or sticks or sacks to sit on," suggested Bromwyn.

"You'd better be in charge of the girls; I'll be in charge of the boys," Nicholas said. "There's to be no fighting. We want evidence, nothing else."

"We know that," snapped James.

"Let's go," Ivor said, thinking, "They're going to quarrel."

The sun had gone now; the day was darkening as they set off along the familiar road.

"Anyone got a piece of paper? We'll need to write down their numbers," Jocelyn said. "I'll go back to the saddle-room."

"We'll wait," Bromwyn answered.

The boys went on. There was a hostile silence between Nicholas and James. Ivor had a knife in his pocket, and a large stone. "If they attack us with bicycle chains and razors, I'll fight back. I don't mean to get my face slashed."

Nicholas had said, "No fighting," he recollected. But that couldn't mean running away if you were attacked, he reasoned.

"There will be a moon later," James said.

"What does that mean?"

"There was a moon last time," James replied patiently.

"So what?"

"You don't ride in the dark," James answered.

"I don't think they'll come anyway. The whole business is a waste of time."

"Why come then?"

They could hear the girls running along the road behind them. In the distance an engine revved up.

"We'd better hurry," James said.

Nicholas lit a cigarette. "We're in plenty of time," he said, turning down the track. "I don't mean to stop long anyway."

"Who's That?"

"The ponies are quite quiet," James said, looking over the gate.

"How many are there?" asked Nicholas.

"Northwind, Dawn and Tango."

"Where are we going to hide?" Ivor asked.

It was quite cold now. Grey clouds moved like smoke across the fading sky. Strange rustles came from the bramble bushes; birds twittered sleepily, like people half-asleep muttering in bed. There was a stillness about everything as though the countryside had already settled itself for the night.

"Behind the bramble bushes I suppose," Nicholas said, stubbing out his cigarette. He couldn't help thinking of home with the long crimson curtains drawn in the drawing-room, his parents watching the film on television, Watchman the Boxer lying at his father's feet.

"We'd better hurry. I'm sure I hear motor-bikes. Listen all of you," Ivor said.

"If we start getting the jitters now, God help us," Nicholas said.

"You don't believe anyone's going to come, do you?" James asked.

"There they go again. They're like two cats fighting in an alley," thought Ivor. "They can't leave off."

He climbed over the bramble bushes, scratching his legs. There was no sound from the road now; even the rustles in the brambles had stopped; then a goods train rattled along the line; a dog started to bark and a voice came from the road:

"Sandra. Come along now. Sandra, do as I tell you."

"Talk about being uncomfortable," complained Nicholas.

"I'm all right," James said.

By the road the girls were hiding too, all together in a field, lying on their tummies chewing blades of grass.

"Do lie on my mac, Stella," Jocelyn said.

"I'm all right thanks," whispered Stella.

"Can you hear the sea?" asked Anne.

"Just."

"I hope they come soon."

"Same here."

"Stella and I will go for the police because we're the fastest runners," Bromwyn said.

"The rest of us will pull those logs there across the track," Jocelyn said, pointing to two old tree trunks lying in the field.

"A good idea. Can you think of any other delaying tactics?" asked Bromwyn.

"Not at the moment. We're not very well equipped."

"I'm getting cold," Stella said.

"Well, we've got hours yet."

"Supposing they don't come at all?"

"Ssh, what was that?"

"Ssh."

"Nicholas is smoking. I can smell it from here," complained Jocelyn a moment later.

"The motor-bike exhausts will be stronger," Bromwyn answered. "The whole place will smell of petrol when they're here."

"When they're here. To think I missed the pops for this," sighed Jocelyn.

"Elvis wasn't on anyway."

"I'm going to try sitting for a bit. What's the time?"

"Five to nine. Have some coffee. We'll have to drink out of the top," said Bromwyn, opening the thermos.

"You know I've hardly had one ride these hols. It isn't fair, is it?" Jocelyn asked.

"Well, that's partly why we're after the gang on motor-bikes, isn't it? If they keep coming none of us will get any more rides because Audrey will give up," replied Bromwyn, imagining the yard empty, and twice as shabby because of that. "When this is over we're going to paint the loose-boxes for Audrey."

"What a super idea."

"Ssh. There's someone coming. Lie flat everybody."

They threw themselves down. Stella upset the half-full thermos; Jocelyn forgot to take off her spectacles. She felt them crack as the lenses hit a stone. "Ssh," hissed Bromwyn.

"He's got a bicycle," whispered Stella.

"Why's there only one?"

"Ssh."

"Are you going for the police?" Jocelyn asked.

"Not yet."

"Can we follow him?"

"We will soon."

They sat up now, their ears listening intently for fresh sounds.

"I hope the boys are well hidden," Anne said.

"There's a light coming down the track. It looks like a bicycle light," Ivor whispered.

"We can see it too, dope," whispered James.

Nicholas ground his cigarette into the earth.

"It's only one. That's not much catch," he said disparagingly.

"More may come," suggested James in a whisper.

"It's probably a labourer taking a short cut home," thought Nicholas. "We'll be able to stop watching soon. With any luck I shall be home in time for the last programmes."

Ivor clutched the stone he carried in his pocket. "Who can it be?" he wondered.

James was disappointed. "He's not even particularly large or old," he thought, "and the bike's a girl's."

The lone figure stopped at the gate, stood looking into the field and listening. Then he seemed to sigh with relief. He turned the bike round and started to walk back.

"That's it," Ivor whispered.

"False alarm," muttered James.

And then they all saw at the same time that the figure was Daniel clad in an unbecoming oilskin mackintosh and sou'wester.

"Daniel," they shouted, leaping over the brambles.

"Why, hullo. So you were here all the time," he said.

The girls were coming down the track to meet them now, creeping, with their shoulders bent.

The moon had risen so that they could see one another quite clearly.

"So it was Daniel all the time," Bromwyn said.

"What a wash-out," exclaimed Stella.

"I thought I might do some sleuthing on my own. I didn't know you would be here. I've spent the whole afternoon persuading a girl to lend me her bike," Daniel explained.

"We may as well go home. I don't suppose anyone is going to come now." Nicholas said. He felt very angry. The whole evening had been wasted. His knees ached from crouching behind the brambles. "It's all very well for the others, you enjoy this sort of thing when you're twelve, but I'm too old for such nonsense," he thought furiously.

"Well, I'm going home," he announced.

"It's hardly half-past nine," Bromwyn said, pushing a dark lock of hair off her face. "Isn't it rather early?"

"Definitely," James agreed.

"Well, I must go. I don't want to be locked out of the hotel or anything. 'Night all," Daniel said.

"Here comes someone else," said Anne.

"Hullo there," called Audrey. "I thought I would come and see how you were getting on."

"We only caught Daniel," Bromwyn said and started to laugh.

"Well, I would call it a day," Audrey said. "Thank you for coming."

"I shall be here again tomorrow night," James answered.

"Same here," Ivor said.

The track was beautiful in the moonlight. Three hedgehogs appeared, snorting and snuffing.

"Aren't they sweet?" cried Stella.

"Five minutes ago you would have imagined them to be a gang on motor-bikes," Jocelyn said.

"One wonders how silly one can get," replied Nicholas.

"I've left the kettle on. Let's have a midnight feast," Audrey suggested.

"Aren't they darlings with their little noses and beady eyes," said Stella looking at the hedgehogs.

The road was almost deserted. "The motor-bikes just don't seem to have come this way tonight. I've been listening all evening," Audrey said.

"I don't believe they will come again," said Nicholas.

"I hope you're right," replied Audrey.

They drank mugs of hot tea and cocoa in Audrey's tiny cottage and munched digestive biscuits.

"Well, I'm going now," said Nicholas quite soon. "Where did I leave my bike?"

"He thinks we're wasting our time," said James when Nicholas had gone.

"He's handsome and handsome people are inclined to get spoilt," Audrey said.

"I'd better go now. I promised Mum and Dad I'd be back soon," Ivor said.

It was ten o'clock now. He knew how it would be at home; his parents still up, watching the door for him, even stepping outside to look up and down the street.

"You all ought to go. Don't bother to help with the washing-up," Audrey said. "It's only mugs anyway."

They all scattered, running across the yard. Ivor took the short cut home across the scrap heap, where bits of old tin and iron, bent cardboard boxes and decaying wood appeared grotesque and ghostly in the moonlight. He could hear the sea in his ears; three cars passed; then he was home, opening the back door, crying, "Sorry I'm late," before he put his nose inside.

His father was snoring in front of the television set. Supper had been cleared away. "Wherever have you been, Ivor?" his mother asked. "We were afraid you had been knocked down or something. Here, have some supper."

"We were watching for the motor-bikes," Ivor began, deciding to tell the truth.

There was soup waiting for Stella, Anne and Bromwyn. Maria came down in her dressing-gown.

"Was it exciting? What happened?" she wanted to know. And Stella was suddenly tired, too tired for anything but bed.

The bungalow was locked when James and Jocelyn reached it; but their mother threw open a window.

"I'll be down in a minute. You *are* late," she said. "Your father is out and I got nervous with only me and Miss Adams in the house. What happened? Here, let me make you a hot drink," she said.

"You are nice, Mummy. We thought you'd be cross and you're not a bit," James said.

"What a nice thing to say to me."

"Audrey made us some cocoa, don't bother, Mummy," Jocelyn said.

"How cold your hands are. Come on both of you, into bed." A wavering voice called, "Are the children back? Oh, I *am* glad."

"She's fond of you, you know," Mrs. Allcott said. "She's been worrying about you all evening."

"I feel like an old piece of limp rag. We only caught Daniel. What a flop and dear Nicholas said as much. He doesn't believe in the gang on motor-bikes at all, Mummy. Do you?" asked James.

"Now stop worrying dear. Everything will look different in the morning," said Mrs. Allcott.

"Bags the bathroom first," Jocelyn said.

"But *do* you Mummy?"

"But James, how should I know?" asked Mrs. Allcott.

Nicholas pedalled slowly home. He was still very angry. He had smoked all his cigarettes, the crease had gone from his trousers and he was hungry; nothing made him crosser than being hungry.

The porch light was on outside the Manse, he saw. So was the garage light. "Why on earth?" he wondered, beginning to cycle faster.

Then he heard his mother call, "Nick, darling, Nick . . ." Next he saw that the paddock gate was open.

"What's happened?" he shouted, standing on the pedals. "Where's Trombone? What's happened, Ma?"

His father was in the road, a halter in his hand.

"I can't find her, Nick," he said. "We heard motor-bikes. We didn't think anything of it. We were watching the play as we always do, you know. Only later Sid from the pub knocked on the door . . ."

"On motor-bikes? You said motor-bikes?" Nicholas asked.

"We heard them revving up. There was some shouting. We didn't think anything of it, Nick. I've been up the road both ways."

Nicholas thought of Patchwork's broken knees, of Jubilee in the pit. "And all the time I was waiting by the wrong gate," he cried. He threw down his bike, and kicked it violently. "I was waiting by the wrong gate, all the time; the whole beastly evening."

"I've rung the police," his father said. "The patrol car's looking out for her and for the motor-bikes. They took some notice, I can tell you."

"What am I to do? Everyone's in bed by this time." Then suddenly Nicholas knew. He picked up his bike again.

"Nick, wait. Wait till morning," his mother shouted.

"I would never sleep," he shouted back. "I couldn't."

How would Trombone look when he found her? He had had so many plans for her; she might never be sound again. She might even be dead by this time. He didn't know where he was going. His feet just turned the pedals, while his mind raced round in a circle with Trombone in the middle of it, dripping blood, and holding up one battered leg.

"It's all my own fault, why didn't I think, why didn't I believe in the gang? Oh, I'm cold," he thought a second later. He had reached a hill. He dismounted. The bright moonlight seemed there to taunt him with misleading shadows, and the road was quite empty. Presently there were hills on each side of him and the road was bordered by stone walls. He turned back.

"Anything may have happened by now," he thought. He was limp; the first sudden rush of uncontrollable anger had left him; now he only experienced despair.

The bicycle ran smoothly down the hill. The moon seemed to be staring straight at him now. All the houses he passed were in darkness save one.

"It feels like midnight," he thought, beginning to pedal again. "How suddenly things happen! Poor Ma, she was so upset. And Pa too."

Perhaps they were waiting up for him. Or they might have heard from the police by this time. Why had he left in such a hurry? He started to pedal faster, faster and faster. He knew the road now; each dent on its surface, each moonlit corner. Then distinctly he heard the clip-clop of hoofs.

He dismounted. His hands were clammy on the handlebars. He was afraid of what he might see. "Perhaps it's Pa and Trombone," he thought; "or the police bringing her home." He rounded the last corner in the winding road leading his bicycle. He saw two youths and behind them limped Trombone.

"He was out. We're bring him home for you," they called. The lights were still on at the Manse, blazing out across the lawn.

"It's a she," replied Nicholas automatically.

The youths had shifty eyes, he saw; but there weren't any motor-bikes to be seen, just the empty moonlit road behind them.

"Where was she? Who are you anyway?" Nicholas said, throwing down his bike.

"You might say thank you, Mister. She was heading for the main road."

"You've been riding her, look at the hair on your jeans," Nicholas shouted.

"Riding her? How? We don't ride."

"Only motor-bikes, I suppose," Nicholas replied with a sneer.

"What's that got to do with you?"

"Quite a lot actually."

"We don't want any of your cheek."

They were taller than Nicholas. They had large, stupid mouths, he saw, and their eyes were stupid too. The larger of the two had a piece of bicycle chain sticking out of one pocket.

"I can't fight them," decided Nicholas. "I must be cunning. If only someone would appear from somewhere. I could do with James now; James and Bromwyn: they would know what to do. Bromwyn would go for the police and James would stay and fight." Then he said, "Well, thanks anyway. Have you got a long way to go?"

"Far enough."

They had made a halter out of rope. Nicholas looked at his mare's legs and saw that her near foreleg was swollen. He knew then that he wouldn't be able to ride her again, not the whole summer holidays, and for a moment he felt overcome with rage. He wanted to throw himself at the two youths who were already walking away down the road. He wanted to shout, to call them names. He controlled himself with difficulty, turned his mare into the paddock, shut the gate and started to follow the youths.

They were walking briskly, their long hair flopping about their necks, their drainpipe trousers covered here and there with Trombone's grey hairs.

Presently he could hear voices calling, "You got back all right then? Come on, let's go." Nicholas was running now. Motor-bike engines started up. There was laughter. He ran and saw the motor-bikes disappearing; five of them, one with a girl on the back. The moonlight didn't show him their numbers; it wasn't light enough for that.

For a long time he stood feeling numb; then he started to walk back along the road.

His father was standing outside the Manse gate, wearing a dressing-gown over his silk pyjamas.

"She's back in the paddock, Nicholas," he called.

"I know. I put her there."

He didn't want to discuss it now when he felt a failure. "She's lame. They've lamed her," he added.

He hurried into the paddock and already the air was that of a new day; the sky was lightening, the moonlight fading.

"I shall have to bathe her leg. She'll need refrigerating lotion I expect. Can I ring the vet in the morning?"

His father came with him.

"We used to hose them in the old days," he said.

"What, with a hosepipe?"

"That's right."

"She's very lame. Shall I put her in the box?"

"I should," his father answered.

"She may be cut. I haven't really looked."

"It looks as though she'd been ridden with a piece of rope in her mouth," Captain Owen said presently, when they had Trombone in the loose-box with the electric light on.

"It's a sprain, isn't it? She may never recover, never be fit for a long day's work again," Nicholas said.

"There's nothing much we can do till morning now. What you need is sleep," Captain Owen said.

"I'll give her a feed. Poor old Trombone," Nicholas replied, pulling the mare's ears. He had a funny feeling in his throat and his head was heavy with anger and fatigue.

He mixed a bucket of bran, oats and chaff.

"Don't be long, Nick," his father called before going indoors.

Nicholas started to wonder about the youths. What were their homes like? Why did they want to torment other people's horses? Was it for pleasure? Or were they seriously trying to learn to ride?

He tipped the bucket of feed into Trombone's manger. She was resting her sprained foreleg. He could see now that she was dirty with dried sweat. Hiding by the gate which led to the bottom meadow seemed to belong to days ago. How bored he had been! If only he had known what was happening to Trombone then!

He switched off the loose-box light. Supper was waiting for him in the kitchen – a thermos jug of hot coffee, cheese, biscuits, fruit. A message read: *There's soup in the simmering oven if you want it*. But he didn't want to eat, and the coffee would keep him awake. He wanted the deep, dreamless sleep of exhaustion so that in the morning he would be ready to find a line of action to follow, to meet the vet, to break the news to the gang of helpers at the riding-school.

His father called, "Are you all right, Nick? Good night then," as he reached the top of the stairs.

"Yes, thanks." He groped his way to his door, found the light.

"What a dreadful day," he thought and his eyes caught the Pony Club fixture card. "All that's finished for me. Perhaps by the autumn she'll be fit to ride again but not before." Seizing the card, he tore it to shreds, stamped on it. "If only I had stayed at home," he thought furiously, "had stayed at home and listened. If only, how I hate those words and always will."

Cocks were crowing now in the distance; birds twittered merrily in the trees outside his window. It was another day already, and he hadn't been to bed at all.

He snatched his clothes off, put on his pyjamas, scrambled into bed. "Poor Trombone," he thought, "Poor little grey Trombone."

A New Plan

First his father's voice was just part of a dream; then it became reality.

"Nick, the vet's here. I telephoned him first thing."

It was long past breakfast-time; Nicholas knew that by the way the sun was shining through the curtains, by the smell of lunch obviously already cooking in the kitchen.

"Coming." He pulled back the curtains and revealed a blue sky, a day too perfect for his own miserable feelings; nothing stirred the trees, the curving sunlit road seemed to call for an artist to paint it; the sea was beating calmly against the rocks, its white foam no more than the bubble of soapflakes in a washing-bowl. The beach was crowded already, and a sail or two moved gently out to sea.

Nicholas dressed quickly. He found the vet, Mr. Harling, with his father in the yard at the back of the house.

"It's a strain, I'm afraid," the vet said.

"Which means months of rest," Nicholas said drearily.

"Well, six weeks anyway. I've left some lotion to be applied. Directions on the bottle."

"As a compress?"

"That's right. Have you got some leg-bandages?"

"Yes."

"Well, I will be off then. She's a nice little mare," Mr. Harling said and Nicholas saw that he was tall, with a stoop and a kind face.

"Will she ever be really sound again?" Nicholas asked.

"Oh yes, I think so. It's a strain, not a sprain. Of course, you must ride her gently at first. It's better to err on the cautious side you know."

"That's rather what I thought."

"Well, good-bye."

"So that's that," said Captain Owen when the vet had gone.

"And we can't sue anyone; because we have no proof that those beastly youths weren't really just bringing Trombone back. Somebody else could have let her out after all," Nicholas said. "But they had her hairs on the legs of their jeans," he added, recalling the whole evening.

He filled Trombone a net of hay, and fetched her clean water.

"Oh Nick, you do look awful. Sit down and have a good breakfast," his mother said when he returned to the house. "We were worried stiff about you last night. Whatever time did you get in? You had better have a quiet day today."

"No thank you. I shan't rest until we catch the youths. I'm going to the riding-school in a minute. If I eat a good breakfast, can I take sandwiches for lunch?"

Bromwyn and Stella were the first of the helpers to arrive at the riding-school. Later Ivor arrived saying, ""I got a telling-off last night from Dad. How about you?"

"I feel like the morning after the night before," replied Bromwyn. "We didn't wake up till nine o'clock, did we, Stella?"

But none of them felt like talking much. They sat about, occasionally getting laboriously to their feet to take a pony, or to answer the telephone.

"I suppose we'll watch again tonight," Ivor said once.

"I suppose so," agreed Browyn.

"I can't," Stella said. "It wouldn't be fair on Mummy. She likes me at home sometimes."

And then suddenly Nicholas arrived, pedalling his bicycle furiously into the yard, looking as though he hadn't combed his hair for a week.

"I believe you all now," he said dismounting, throwing his bicycle down.

The others didn't move; only Bromwyn said "Why?" without much interest in her voice.

"You look like a lot of cabbages," cried Nicholas contemptuously. "Look, they *did* come last night. They rode Trombone."

"No!" cried Bromwyn. "Oh, Nick, I'm sorry."

"She's lame. I suppose they galloped her on the road. She won't be sound again the whole holidays."

James and Jocelyn were coming into the yard now.

"What's the matter?" James cried.

"The gang have got at Trombone," Ivor shouted.

They all clustered round Nicholas listening to his story. The day seemed to grow hotter; hotter and hotter as Nicholas's temper rose and they stood there listening.

"Ma's gone into town to buy a couple of padlocks. We're going to padlock the loose-box door. Pa's guarding Trombone," Nicholas finished.

"What about the police?" James asked. "You said your father telephoned the police."

"What were they like? Would you know them again?" demanded Bromwyn.

"They must have something against us. They must know Jim Morgan," Ivor said.

"Let's go into the saddle-room. I'm so hot," said Nicholas. "The police are sitting up a bit at last. They're beginning to prick their ears. Of course, they know Pa's name and that makes a difference. They can't accuse *him* of being an alarmist," he said when he was sitting down in the one and only saddle-room chair.

"Would you know the youths again?" repeated Bromwyn standing in the doorway. "Could you pick them out at an identity parade?"

"Well, the light wasn't very good; but I think I could."

"You didn't see their motor-bikes?" asked James.

"Well hardly."

"What are we going to do?" asked Stella.

"Yes, what *are* we going to do?" repeated Bromwyn.

"Here's the ride coming back," James said, going out into the yard, thinking, "This is it. We know for certain that the gang exists now. Nicholas is with us now to the hilt."

"Trombone's been lamed now," Bromwyn said, taking Audrey's mount.

"Oh, no! Nicholas, I am sorry," Audrey said. "We've got to do something now. We'll have to set up a patrol," James said in a tight voice.

"You can borrow a pony if you like," Audrey answered.

"Thank you."

"Here's Daniel," Nicholas said.

"I'll tell him," offered Bromwyn. "You must be sick of telling people, Nick."

"After lunch we'll meet in the granary. All right?" Nicholas asked.

"All right," agreed James.

They helped Audrey feed and water the ponies. Nicholas swept the yard and gradually the motion of the broom and the quietness of the munching horses soothed him. "We will catch them somehow," he thought, "and take them to the police station and they'll be charged for trespass and damage and with cruelty to animals. I hope they go to Borstal."

"Dad will forgive me if I tell him what happened last night. He'll know I'm on the right side, the side of law and order," Ivor thought. "I must be in the patrol. No one is going to stop me, nobody."

"We'll have to patrol every night, won't we?" asked James when they met again, sitting once more in the granary.

"We'll have to take it in turns then," Bromwyn said.

"James is right. We can't afford to miss a night. Until we catch them, no horse is safe. I can't keep Trombone in for ever. Think of the hay bills."

"It's the same for Audrey. She can't afford to do without the bottom meadow," Bromwyn answered.

"Nightly patrol," Jocelyn wrote on a piece of paper. "We'll need a rota system," she said.

"What's that?" asked Stella.

"She means take it in turns," explained James.

"And we must be properly equipped, and there must be two of us at least. I hadn't a chance against the two I met. What could I do?" asked Nicholas.

"They've got a nerve doing it so near a house. I mean your paddock is next to your house, isn't it?" asked Daniel, who had turned up uninvited as usual.

Nicholas nodded. "I think they did it like this: first they opened the gate (so that they could truthfully say they found her out) ; then when she was out of sight of the house they caught her. You see the man in the pub saw her walking along the road on her own. He ran to the Manse to tell my parents but when Pa started to look for her she seemed to have disappeared from the face of the earth."

"It's really ghastly, isn't it? I mean I'm really quite glad I haven't got a horse around here," Daniel said.

"Let's get back to the patrols. Are we going to have a boy and a girl each time?" asked Ivor.

"I think we had better talk the whole thing over with our parents first. Audrey says she'll keep the bottom meadow ponies in the paddock tonight, it'll mean feeding hay of course, since there isn't a blade of grass. Nick will keep Trombone's stable door padlocked. We could all do with sleep," Bromwyn said.

"Hear hear," said James.

"I certainly could, I'm feeling half dead. Gosh, I could have killed those youths last night. I had to keep myself on a pretty tight rein, I can tell you."

"Let's adjourn until tomorrow then," Jocelyn suggested.

"And spend this evening using our brains," Bromwyn answered.

"Yes. Could we, for instance, tether some of Audrey's ponies up on the old common next Friday night. There's gorse bushes all round, and the sea on one side. Surely tethered ponies would tempt them more than anything else?" suggested Daniel.

"Gosh, that's a super idea! Dan, you're a genius," cried James.

"Do they tether though?" asked Stella.

"Come on, let's ask Audrey."

They tumbled out of the granary, Stella grazing her knees on the wooden ladder.

"Audrey, Audrey," called James.

"Whatever's happened?" she cried, appearing from the cottage.

"Do any of your ponies tether?" asked Nicholas.

"Daniel's had a smashing idea," chimed in Ivor.

"Yes, a few. I tethered a few the year before when there was a drought and hardly any grass to be had anywhere. I've still got the tethering-pegs somewhere."

"Hurray," shouted James, dancing round the yard.

"We want to tether them on the common," explained Nicholas.

"That's where I tethered them then," Audrey replied.

"Friday had better be the night," James said.

"It's a long time away," grumbled Ivor.

"I'll keep them in the paddock at the back until then," Audrey said. "I can watch them from my bedroom window and I'll leave the dogs out until midnight. The ponies should be safe then."

"Oh, I'm hot," grumbled Jocelyn.

"We won't bother then till Friday," Bromwyn said. "Let's start cleaning the tack."

"Will you still be here on Friday, Dan?" James asked.

"Yes, just. Mother, Rosemary and I are here for a month. Father's gone back. I don't know how I would have survived without this place. I'm a bit old for sand-castles on the beach."

"I'm going now," Nicholas said, pedalling out of the drive.

"Poor Nick, it's a shame about Trombone," Bromwyn said, starting to clean a saddle.

"I'm so hot," grumbled Jocelyn again.

"We've got to go home for lunch. I shall swim later," James said.

"How's Maria?" Ivor asked.

"Getting crosser and crosser. Mummy won't let her come here. She says she would be certain to forget about her neck and start riding or sweeping the yard."

"What about Dobbin and the church fête? When are we going to find a home for him? We can't possibly feed him through another winter," James said.

They started to discuss the Shire horse, while the day grew hotter; until James said, "It's time for us to go home, Jocelyn."

The road was hot under their feet.

"I bet it's sausages and mash for lunch," James said.

"How do you know?"

"I saw the sausages in the larder. Doesn't Friday seem years and years away?"

"Not too long. I could do with a few restful days."

They were home now. The kitchen smelt of cooking and gas, mixed evenly.

"I wish Miss Adams would go. Then we could have the sitting-room back," James said.

"Mummy must be at the post office. I'll lay the table," Jocelyn said.

James sank into the only comfortable chair. "These holidays seem to have lasted for years and years already," he exclaimed.

This Is The Day

Once more it was Friday. Stella had arranged to stay with the Fishers again. Miss Adams had gone, so the sitting-room in the bungalow was free again and Mrs. Allcott was better-tempered, and the endless trips to the post office were over for Jocelyn and James.

To all the helpers at the riding-school it had seemed a long week. Nicholas had mourned over Trombone; he had gone to bed each night imagining the things he would have done during the day had Trombone been sound. He had been in a constant state of anger. He had swum furiously, battling against waves, pitting his strength against the sea, he had cut the nettles in the paddock ferociously, had mown the lawn, creosoted the outside of the garden shed, but his anger had stayed smouldering inside him like a fire inside a volcano.

His parents were exasperated.

"Listen, Nick darling. We know it's sickening about Trombone. But you know we all have our troubles in life. We have to accept them; it's no good going about like a wounded lion," Mrs. Owen said wearily on a hot afternoon, when thunder rumbled in the distance and Nicholas was angrily mowing the lawn, with sweat running off his face, and his head aching.

"I can't help it. I hate them. Why should they do these terrible things to other people's horses? We don't smash up their motor-bikes. Why should they get away with it?" he demanded, still pushing the mower, as though the mower was one of the youths whom he was frogmarching across the lawn.

"But the police are looking out for them."

"Oh, the police. They aren't treating it seriously. Constable Wilson's an oaf," Nicholas replied.

Trombone was still lame; it angered Nicholas every time he looked at her resting her swollen foreleg. He knew how a strain might keep coming back; how she might never be fit for cross country work unless he was very careful. And he didn't want to be careful. He wanted to ride her in the trials in the autumn as he had planned.

"They've mucked up my whole summer if you want to know," he said angrily to his mother.

"But do you only care about riding? Can't you do your underwater swimming, or practise cricket?"

"Who with?"

"James or someone."

But he didn't want to be happy, not with Trombone lame and the youths uncaught; he went on raging about the house until Friday came. Then suddenly he was cool and calm and ready for anything.

"I need a notebook, a pencil and some pennies for a telephone call," he announced at lunch. "This is the night. Can I take some sandwiches with me? I'll padlock Trombone's doors top and bottom."

"And we'll leave Watchman out. You'll let us know if anyone trespasses, won't you old fellow?" Captain Owen asked his dog.

"And be careful, Nick. you know what teddy-boys can be like. They may have knives or razors," Mrs. Owen pleaded.

"We don't mean to fight them. We just want them caught. Audrey's going to let the police know where the ponies are and the patrol car should be cruising round most of the night."

"Good luck," his father said, before Nicholas cycled away after lunch, wearing trousers, open-necked shirt, hacking jacket and plimsolls. He had his cap pulled over one eye, as usual.

Trombone was neighing in her stable. She hadn't liked being padlocked in, though Nicholas had told her repeatedly, "I'm not doing this for fun; it's for your own safety. I'm sorry." He had tried to soothe her with carrots, but without success, for it was obvious she hated the top door shut. She was still limping round the box when he left; limping and limping and each limp hurt Nicholas and made him all the more determined to catch the youths who lamed her.

Ivor helped his mother wash up the midday meal as usual. But it wasn't like a usual day. He had his parents' blessing. "Go and good luck," they had said when he had asked permission for another late night. He had put them in the picture by this time and they knew whom he would be with. "But you're not to take any weapons, Ivor, you understand, don't you?" his mother had insisted.

All the same he meant to fill his pockets with a few stones, and in his shirt pocket he had a knife.

"Expect me when you see me then, Mum," he said, hanging up a tea-towel.

"Aren't you going rather early?"

"We've got to tether the ponies. And I want to give Audrey a hand with the tack," Ivor replied, taking off his sandals to replace them with black plimsolls.

"They're a spot quieter," he smiled at his mother.

"Oh, you are a lad!" she exclaimed and kissed him. "You're like my brother was – always in a scrape."

"But this isn't just a scrape," thought Ivor walking along the road, past two notices which read, *Bed and Breakfast*. "It's serious. More like a war."

He started to whistle. "Well, they won't be able to ride Trombone tonight," he thought. "She's under lock and key. I wish there were more boys among us and less girls. Still the girls are all right and Bromwyn can run faster than most boys if it comes to that."

He met Nicholas on his bike as he neared the stable. "We're both early," Nicholas said.

"Better early than late," replied Ivor.

"Now mind you eat up all these sandwiches, James. You know what the doctor said, and you're not any fatter at all. Don't give them away to the other children. I can't feed the whole riding-school, you know," Mrs. Allcott said, handing them each a large package. "Now what about something to drink?"

"Squash please," James said. He had hardly slept all night. "It's tomorrow," he kept thinking, "this time tomorrow we will be waiting, watching. They must come this time; and later, it will be over by this time." Far away a clock had struck midnight and then the solitary hour of one. He was tired now, though he had slept till past nine, tired and on edge, but ready at the same time to fight if necessary.

"Come on, Jocelyn," he said. He was wearing plimsolls, for they had all agreed on that, that and a good many other things.

"I refuse to run. We're in plenty of time. It's scorching hot. What's the point of getting exhausted for nothing?" demanded Jocelyn, who had slept like a top.

"You only say that because you can't keep up," retorted James.

"Well, you run if you like. I don't care. I've got a lot to carry."

"I should say you have. What's in the bag?" asked James noticing that his sister carried a shopping-bag.

"It's secret."

"Oh, all right." James started to run, out of habit. The melting tar on the road stuck to his plimsolls; then small pebbles stuck to the tar.

Jocelyn nursed the shopping-bag. "I bet no one else has thought of bringing a camera; of course, it was Daddy's idea really," she remembered. "Why must James always run? Everybody looks at him. The older he grows the sillier it looks," she decided.

Jocelyn had always hated to be looked at. For that reason she never ate in the street, nor in a bus, never munched an apple as she walked along the road, didn't run in a crowd unless she was forced to. "The Fishers are the same now," she decided; "people are always looking at them, particularly Maria."

During the last few weeks Jocelyn had been keeping a diary. She had already written *Friday* on it. *Packed camera in shopping bag, Mummy made us sandwiches. Left after lunch for the stables*. She had the diary with her now, for she meant to record the whole evening in it; she couldn't help feeling it might be useful later on, for in a way surely it would count as evidence. Evidence! The camera was to record the night too, if there was moonlight and the weather-man had forecast a bright night. For once in her life Jocelyn meant to shine. She could see her brother turning into the stable-yard now, still running as though his life depended on it. She felt quite cool in her shorts and pink cotton blouse. "James must be boiling by now," Jocelyn decided, feeling smug and sensible.

"Good-bye darling. Have a nice stay. I shouldn't bother about not being able to talk to Mr. Fisher. I'll see you tomorrow for lunch," Stella's mother said. Breakfast was washed up and cleared away. She was wearing her office clothes – a slim dress, a double row of pearls and medium-heeled, black shoes.

"You've been jolly decent about the whole thing, Mummy," Stella said.

"Well, good-bye, darling, I must fly. Be careful." They kissed and Stella was alone with the morning to pass before the next bus to the Seashore School of Equitation.

This was one of those days when she longed for a brother or sister, or at least a dog. She didn't feel like reading; it was too early for television. She sat on the window-ledge, watching the people passing along the street. She thought about the evening and suddenly it seemed very near. "If only I lived in the country. I could go for walks then; but who wants to walk in a town?" she thought.

In the end she read a pony book and at twelve o'clock she ate her lunch and washed up. There was still an hour until the next bus was due in the busy main street. All the same she put on her riding-jacket, combed her hair, shut her suitcase, checked that the gas-cooker was off, locked the doors. "I'll walk about for a bit," she thought, running down the stairs.

But it was still the lunch-hour in the town and all the shops were shut. "How slowly time passes when one is alone," thought Stella; "yet at the riding-school it seems to fly far too quickly." She could see her reflection in shop windows – straight yellow hair, a round face, checked riding-jacket, jeans, scarlet socks and plimsolls. She hadn't wanted to take the jacket, but her mother had insisted; now she was far too hot. At last the green country bus came. Stella sat in the front imagining life in a family; imagining that her sister sat beside her now, saying, "Isn't that a pretty cottage? Look Stella, horse."

Presently the bus was full and Stella stood up to give her seat to an elderly woman loaded with two shopping-bags. It was very hot; there seemed no air in the bus at all now; and every time it stopped Stella fell against the man in front of her. But finally it reached the familiar stop and she was out on the road, smelling the sea, thinking, "This is the day."

For some reason she thought she would find the yard changed in some subtle way, but it was just the same – the horses nodding over their loose-box doors, Audrey with her arms full of tack, the guinea fowls scratching round the granary, the dogs sunning themselves.

"Why can't I go?" shouted Maria. "I missed last time. My silly neck is quite all right in this plaster.

What can happen to it, I ask you? Please let me go, please, please."

"You are not going," replied Mrs. Fisher.

Tears began to roll down Maria's cheeks, large tears for whatever Maria did she did in a big way.

"It does seem hard," said Anne, packing sandwiches into a paper bag.

"But it's your own fault really. Why must you rush in where angels fear to tread?" asked Bromwyn.

"I don't know what you mean," retorted Maria, blowing her nose.

"Well, fall down the pit. Why didn't you look before you leapt?"

"I don't jump my fences before I come to them," answered Maria.

"That's not the same thing."

"Yes, it is."

"No, it isn't."

The builders were coming up the path, carrying the inevitable ladder and great tins of paint.

"Stop arguing. Here come the builder's men. I'm sorry for you, Maria," Anne said.

"Here's your thermos, Bromwyn. We all have our bad patches in life; it will pass. Better miss tonight than have a stiff neck for ever, Maria sweetheart," said Mrs. Fisher.

"But there may never be another night like tonight," Maria shouted.

Bromwyn lifted the latch on the back door.

"Well, good-bye. Come on, Anne," she said.

The garden was ruined by the lorries which had been over it; only a few tall hollyhocks remained in the border which last year had been crowded with a mass of flowers. The new studio showed a corner of glass to the rough hills at the back.

"Sometimes I wish Daddy hadn't grown rich and famous. The cottage was much cosier before and oh, how tired I am of everything being topsy-turvy," Anne said.

"It won't go on for ever. Look at that hill over there, look at the light. You know I haven't done any painting these holidays," Bromwyn grumbled.

"But we're doing something for other people. That's important, isn't it?" replied Anne.

"I suppose so. But I'm not unselfish like you."

"But you're fond of Nicholas."

"Yes, I am."

The seven of them sat about making plans until the afternoon class started in the paddock. There were bending-poles to be put up, jumps to be altered. The ground was softer now, though with the sun blazing down, it would soon be hard again.

"Perhaps Audrey will be able to book us two rides each next week," James said hopefully.

Jocelyn sat nursing her shopping-bag until Nicholas asked, "What on earth have you got in there, Jocelyn? The way you're holding it it might be a baby."

"It's a camera – Daddy's. I want to snap the gang, if there's enough light," she answered.

"What, as evidence?" Nicholas asked.

"What a smashing idea!" exclaimed Ivor.

"But will it be light enough?" asked Bromwyn.

"Are you any good with a camera? Perhaps you'd better let me have it," Nicholas suggested.

"I can manage it," Jocelyn said and then, thinking quickly, she added, "Daddy made me promise not to let anyone else use it." This was not, of course, true but Jocelyn said to herself, "Daddy wouldn't want Nicholas to use it, so it's almost the truth."

"I wish I had thought of bringing one," Nicholas said. "After all, you needn't tell your father that you let me borrow it."

"He wouldn't like it," Jocelyn replied firmly. "He

They sat about making plans

might ask. Then I should have to tell a lie."

"Oh well, if you feel like that about it. But it's going to be pretty disappointing for the rest of us, if you bosh the whole thing," Nicholas said.

"Do leave her alone, Nick. It was her idea in the first place. Nobody else had such a good idea, so why shouldn't she have the fun of taking the photographs?" asked Anne.

"It's too hot to tether the ponies yet. I'm afraid you'll have to wait until half-past four at least," Audrey said after she had announced the end of the class.

"That suits us fine. We don't want to sit for hours and hours behind the gorse-bushes. I wish I had brought a chess-board," Nicholas answered. "Can you play chess, Bromwyn? I learned at my prep school."

"No."

"I'll teach you one of these days, though girls aren't generally much good at it."

The ponies filed through the gate into the hot, waiting yard. There wasn't a cloud anywhere in the endless blue of the sky. The dogs had gone inside to lie in Audrey's brick-floored kitchen.

"I'll take Tango," Ivor said.

Bromwyn fetched a bucket of warm water from the kitchen, found the sponges and started to wash the dirty tack.

"I needn't clean tack, need I, Audrey? I get enough tack-cleaning with Trombone's," asked Nicholas, sitting in the saddle-room getting in everyone's way, except when he took Mr. Allcott's camera out into the yard.

Returning it to Jocelyn he said, "I took a photo of the ponies with it. You needn't tell your father I took it. It's a super camera. Do you understand all the gadgets?"

"You are the limit," Anne said, wondering what

Bromwyn saw in Nicholas besides his fair, obvious good looks.

"Well, do you, Jocelyn?" he insisted, standing in front of her.

"You shouldn't take things belonging to other people without asking their permission," Audrey said.

"Oh, all right." He handed Jocelyn the camera, went back to the hot yard, lit himself a cigarette and thought, "I'm getting too old for this place. Girls like Jocelyn get on my nerves. As for Anne one would never think she came from the same family as Bromwyn."

The tack was finished now.

"I'll get you the tethering-pegs and rope and the beetle to hammer them in with," Audrey said.

"We can make our final plans when we get there," James said to no one in particular.

It was five o'clock when they set off, Nicholas riding blue roan Northwind, Ivor on Tango, Jocelyn on chestnut Firecracker, and James on Dawn. The others had lost the toss and were walking. The hottest part of the day was over but the beach was still seething with people, the road full of cars from which children leaned, crying, "Look at the ponies, aren't they sweet?"

"Poor Maria, how she would have liked to be here," Anne thought, carrying a coil of rope.

Stella was thinking of her mother returning to the flat. She carried a tethering-peg and her jacket, while Jocelyn had the precious camera slung over her shoulder. James had a knife, and two pockets full of sugar, since he was planning to put sugar in the petrol-tanks of the motor-bikes, if he could find the petrol-tanks and had time; otherwise the sugar would be divided equally between the four ponies.

There were picnickers on the common when they reached it.

"Oh heck," Bromwyn said.

"We needn't tether them just where they are," Nicholas said.

They could see the beach below clearly now. The sea was still going out; the sands looked long and golden where they weren't crowded with people. Between the strip of common and the sands were the sand-dunes, where two ladies sat knitting and an old man read his evening paper.

On two sides of the common were gorse-bushes still in bloom. The grass was wiry, particularly near the sand-dunes. The children stood looking. "This is important. Where are we going to hide?" James asked.

"Which way will they come?" asked Anne.

"Along the road from the town, I suppose," Stella said.

The picnickers were looking at them now. The old man folded his paper before standing up. The ladies looked at them and went on knitting.

"Well, let's dismount, anyway," Nicholas said.

They threw down the stakes and ropes.

"Now do you remember exactly what Audrey said?" asked Nicholas. "I wasn't listening."

"As usual," replied Anne.

"That's nothing new," James said. "We are to tether the ponies with a few feet between each of them when the ropes are taut. We are to make sure they can't get entangled in bushes, eat anything poisonous or reach the road."

"And we're to knock the stakes right in," added Jocelyn.

"And we're to make sure there's no broken glass about, or old tins. I'll start looking now," said Ivor.

"James and I will knock in the stakes," Nicholas told the others.

"Let's get started then. It's nearly half-past five already," James replied.

"I Wish They Would Come"

"That's the lot," said James, banging in the last of the iron stakes.

"Do you really think they'll come so early?" Nicholas asked.

"No."

"Not likely."

"Not a hope."

"Let's sit among the sand-dunes. Then we'll look like everybody else if they do happen to come before the moon rises," Bromwyn suggested.

"It's risen already, look," Ivor exclaimed. They could all see a pale moon hovering in the sky while the sun still blazed red and gold above the sea.

"It's a wonderful evening. Let's share out what grub we have and picnic. We may not have a chance to eat later," said James.

People were leaving the beach now in a steady stream; small children trailed their parents crying, "Wait, Mummy, wait."

"I suppose we were like that once," Anne said.

"It's difficult to believe, isn't it?" asked Nicholas.

"I'm sure I was even worse," Bromwyn said.

The two knitters folded their knitting carefully, placed it in emboidered bags and went away. A boy came over the dunes carrying a bucket of shells. Gradually, slowly, there was silence on the beach below except for the waves idly lapping the sand.

"It's quiet now, like it is in autumn," decided James. "What an evening for a swim!" He knew how it would be in the bed-and-breakfast places: tired children eating a cooked tea, spilling bits and pieces on the tablecloths; while in the hotels the more sophisticated people would be moving towards the bar for their first drink of the evening. "Where's Daniel?" he wondered. "He's too young for a bar. Perhaps he sits upstairs in the elegant bedroom, or reads glossy magazines in the splendid lounge."

"What about photographing the scene, Jocelyn?" suggested Nicholas.

"All right." She stood up, pushed her spectacles more firmly on to her nose and took the camera out of its case. Anne started to screw up the lid on the thermos jug again and pick up paper.

"They may come soon. Don't you think we ought to hide?" asked James. "There aren't many people about just now, are there? I mean it's the dinner and tea hour. A good time for them to strike surely?" And, as if to back him up, a motor-cycle roared in the distance and they all ran for cover.

"It's only one," he said. "How are we going to hide?" And suddenly James felt in command as he had once before when they had battled with Jim Morgan. He knew what to do, could imagine the motor-bikes arriving, their engines roaring, then gradually subsiding, so that the voices of their riders could be heard.

"We need someone near the road. Someone who can go for the police at once. It had better be a girl," he added.

"It had better be Bromwyn; she had better be on the other side of the road," Nicholas said.

"Let's find a place."

"Can't there be two people?" Stella asked.

"The more people there are the more noise they will make; the gang musn't know there's anyone on the other side," James said.

Across the road was a field full of thistles and ragwort. Fenced with wire, it had no cover at all.

"Oh dear," exclaimed Bromwyn.

"Could she hide by the sand-dunes and then edge her way round?" asked Anne.

"We ought to have considered all this before," said Nicholas.

"We ought to have visited here yesterday," agreed James. "All the same, the sand-dunes at the side leading to the road seem the best bet. What do you think, Bromwyn?"

"Yes. I can skulk. I'm used to hills and rough paths. I shall be all right."

"Perhaps Stella should go with you and stay there as a second chance. Then if you are seen you can reveal yourself happily and she can go later when everybody's looking the other way," James suggested.

"It suits me," Stella said.

Nicholas lit himself a cigarette. "James is taking charge as usual, cocky devil," he thought. The two girls disappeared behind the sand-dunes, while the rest of the party dispersed among the gorse.

"Listen everybody. We won't accost the group until they have the ponies untied; that will give Bromwyn time to get away. Then we must hold the gang in conversation. I think we should try to encircle them but not aggressively. What do you think, Nicholas?" James asked.

"I agree. We must avoid a fight at all costs. Yet they must actually be on or holding the ponies when the police arrive."

"Which means we must wait until the last possible moment really, until Jocelyn has taken the photographs and they've put their beastly bits of string and bicycle chains on the ponies."

"Yes, they *must* be still here. Otherwise they can pretend again that they found the ponies straying."

"Exactly."

"What a lot there is to it. I wish Maria was here," Ivor whispered to Anne.

"The strongest of us had better be near the road; the youngest with their backs to the sea," James said.

"I'm the youngest, aren't I? I'll move over there near the dunes," Ivor said.

"Jocelyn and Anne can support him on the two sides. Jocelyn, be ready with that camera for pity's sake. Don't bosh it whatever you do," Nicholas said.

"I won't." Jocelyn's hand was shaking now. She hadn't meant to take on so much. For the first time she started to examine the camera fully but was unable to read the numbers or understand the arrows on it because of the faintness of the evening light.

Ivor collapsed behind a gorse-bush; he was hungry now; was missing the cooked tea he usually had at home at six o'clock. "I wish Maria was here," he kept thinking. "Jocelyn's so stuffy and Anne's all right, but she's not like Maria, hasn't got the life in her somehow." He could just see the ponies, grazing peacefully. "When they start raising their heads, I'll know something's up, motor-bikes or not," he decided.

Among the sand-dunes Stella said, "I hope we don't have to wait too long."

"But we couldn't have a lovelier place to wait. Look at the sea. And the beach is quite empty now. I wish I hadn't drunk so much of James's squash. I'm sure I won't be able to run a yard. I'm not really much of a runner," Bromwyn replied.

And now the sun had gone and the moon still rode pale as the whitest yellow in the sky which had become grey, half-way between evening and night.

"They must come soon," Stella said.

"They may not come at all."

"But they must if they're coming from the town."

"That's true."

"I hate waiting. I'm always waiting at home. Honestly. Waiting for Mummy to come home, waiting

He could see the ponies, grazing peacefully

for the bus, waiting to catch the laundry-man on Saturdav mornings," Stella said.

Nicholas lit himself another cigarette, his last. "They'd better come soon," he thought, "I'm not waiting here for ever." And he remembered Trombone limping round her box and wondered dismally whether she had stopped yet. He pushed his cap back on his head and thought about what he would do with the rest of the holidays when the loathsome gang was caught and prosecuted. Perhaps he would stay with John Manton in Somerset, or stay at home and improve his water skiing. He might ask Bromwyn to go to the theatre with him.

There was a noisy engine coming along the road now and he strained his ears to diagnose its throb. Ancient Baby Austin he decided and at the same time James called, "Baby Austin," which made him furious. Next there was a lorry crashing its brakes as it slowed down for the corner; then a car full of laughing people which made him alert for a moment; then silence again except for the cry of a gull and the endless, inevitable sound of the sea.

"How many will there be?" he wondered. "Will the boys have their girl friends with them? I shouldn't be here really; because the youths who took Trombone may recognise me." This hadn't occurred to him before; now the folly of appearing struck him with force.

"James, James, I shall have to stay hidden. They'll recognise me. They know me," he said and he was filled with anguish.

"I hadn't thought of that."

"They'll know we're in earnest if they see me. Besides I'm nearer their age. You'll seem just a pack of busy-bodying children. But people are always taking me for eighteen."

"You'll have to be in reserve then. That doesn't leave many," James said. "Jocelyn, Ivor, Anne and me–four."

"Better to have a few. We don't want them to be scared and flit."

"You're dead right," James replied, his voice suddenly full of admiration.

"Of course, they may not come at all."

"Of course. But listen. . . ."

"I can't hear anything."

"Can't you?"

"Oh, come on, it's only a train."

Three or four cars passed along the road; someone was singing in one of them and another one needed a new silencer, Nicholas decided. The evening seemed even quieter now. There had been flies earlier but they had gone now. The ponies had stopped eating and stood idly resting legs. Even the sea seemed somehow quieter and the gulls had gone.

"Mum and Dad will be watching Telly now; it's boxing tonight. What will your parents be doing, Anne?" asked Ivor.

"Not so loud. Daddy will be in the studio. Maria will be going to bed. Mummy, well, I don't know about Mummy. One never knows with Mummy. She may be with Daddy, or ironing, or sitting in the garden, or making jam," whispered Anne.

"I wish they would come," Ivor said.

"Not my parents?"

"No, the gang on motor-bikes of course."

"It's so quiet here. I'm not used to quiet. At home there's always traffic outside. When I'm alone I generally switch on the radio or television."

"Listen," said Bromwyn. "Don't speak. Don't move, listen."

"They're coming," Nicholas whispered. "I wish I could go out and meet them. Oh God, I do."

"Can you hear anything, Anne?"

"Yes, motor-bikes."

"Get the camera ready, Jocelyn."

"All right. All right. Now I've dropped it."

It wasn't quite dark yet; not dark enough for the moon to light the sky. The silence had gone, a gull cried, sheep baa-ed and in the distance there was a low, spluttering roar.

Ivor's hands tightened on the stones in his pocket. Jocelyn's hands searched the prickly gorse for the camera. James bit his nails, his whole body tense, his heart hammering against his ribs.

"They're coming," Stella said, because she wanted to hear a voice and be sure she wasn't alone yet among the sand-dunes.

"Shut up," snapped Bromwyn.

The engines slowed down. Strong lights lit up the common. The ponies raised their heads. They shifted their legs; the whole common was alert.

"This is it," James said and was suddenly immeasurably glad that fate had brought them the gang so soon.

"Well, here we are. Come on, what are we waiting for?" cried a voice. "Who wants which? Speak up or for ever hold your peace."

Nicholas was certain he knew the voices. The lights were switched off; heavy feet moved through the grass, followed by pointed shoes, female jeans.

"Oh, Terry, you must have that one," called a girl's voice.

"What do you mean *must*? Who's boss here?"

The voice was arrogant. Ivor was suddenly afraid. James thought, "Not yet, not yet."

Silently, Bromwyn left the dunes. Crawling behind the motor-bikes slung on their sides on the common, she reached the road; then she was running, running, while James's orange squash went up and down inside her. She was afraid to look back. She could only run on towards the telephone kiosk which she knew stood at the next corner but one, brightly lit, the end of her commission.

Stella stayed listening among the dunes. She didn't raise her head, only listened and the strange voices continued talking, lively and aggressive.

"All right, you have that one, Terry. I'll have the brown one over there. Handy them being tied up, ain't it?"

"Don't waste time. We need to get away from here. Got the chains?" And then, "Open your mouth. You brute. . . ."

"I bet you can't ride that one, Al," called a girl's voice.

"How much do you bet? Come on, how much?"

A bird left the gorse, flying away over the ponies' heads with frightened, flapping wings.

Bromwyn could see the kiosk now; her right hand searched her pocket for four pennies, before she realised that she wouldn't need pennies, that she would only need to pick up the receiver and say, "Police."

The Gang

"How does one get on the thing? Stand still, will you?"

"Jump, Terry. Come on, be a man."

Nicholas writhed, remembering Trombone lame, limping along the road covered with sweat.

A girl pushed a tall boy with dark hair on to Firecracker. "Hurry up, the rest of you," he cried.

"He's got long hair. What a sight he looks," thought Stella, raising her head for a moment to peer at the youths and girls among the ponies on the suddenly moonlit common.

"What was that?" shouted a youth.

"Don't ask me. Didn't I say hurry. The riders will be here soon."

"Who cares? They couldn't fight to save their lives,

poor wet things. They need their noses wiped for them even that . . ."

"Well, they put poor old Jim Morgan inside, didn't they?"

"We're the riders," thought James. "We're the riders and any minute now we're going into battle. Another moment and they'll all be mounted. . . ."

Bromwyn reached the kiosk. The moon was shining now, transforming everything. She saw there was a man inside. He was wearing a raincoat; beside him was a pile of pennies. A car passed lighting up his lean features and the cigarette dangling from one corner of his mouth.

"Can you hurry, please? It's urgent," cried Bromwyn.

"So's mine."

He put down the receiver, started dialling all over again.

"How long will you be?" shouted Bromwyn. She looked for a house; but there wasn't one, only a twisty, moonlit road and on the left of it the grey slag-heaps.

"Please hurry!" she begged, thinking all the while. "They'll be on the ponies now. Oh, I hope Jocelyn's photographed them. Surely that will count as evidence."

On the common Jocelyn had the camera ready. She daren't stand up yet, not until James or Nicholas moved or gave a sign. Her hands kept shaking, and her back ached from crouching. "I'll never forget this, not as long as I live," she thought. And over on the other side of the common Ivor was thinking the same thing.

"Bromwyn must have reached the kiosk by now, she must have," decided Anne.

"Come on, let's go," said Terry. At the same time James calmly walked into the open. There was a click of a camera and Jocelyn was standing feeling calm and capable as she prepared to take another photograph.

"Hi, what's this?" cried Al. James saw that he had thick arms, suede shoes, long hair, a faded grey shirt, and trousers which could do with a crease.

"I don't want to be unpleasant but are these your ponies? I just wondered that's all," James asked.

"Haven't I seen you somewhere before, youngster; haven't I?" Terry asked.

Ivor and Anne were moving up now. Jocelyn took another photograph.

"Hi, one of you girls, smash that camera. Go on, get it," yelled Al.

Everyone seemed to be chasing Jocelyn now.

"Here, give it to me," whispered Nicholas and suddenly she was free of it, running round the gorse, over the sand-dunes, empty-handed. Two girls in jeans, thick sweaters and crash-helmets were in hot pursuit.

"Go on, catch her, go on," screamed Terry. "We'll smash it when we get it and throw it in the sea. Come on, boys, let's go. The girls can catch us up."

Leaving the camera hidden in the gorse, Nicholas stepped out then. "Hullo. Haven't we met before?" he asked.

Stella ran to help Jocelyn struggling among the sand-dunes without her spectacles. "She ain't got it, Al. She ain't got it," yelled the tallest girl.

"Where are the police?" wondered James. "What's happened to Bromwyn?"

There were five youths and three girls he saw now, and they all looked as though they could fight, not fairly as he had been taught, but with kicks in the face, in the stomach, with hidden weapons and broken bottles.

"Where is it? Come on, where is it?" yelled Terry. James knew then that he was the leader. Firecracker was wearing a bicycle chain in his mouth, attached to his ears by string.

"You think you're clever, don't you?" Terry shouted

at James and Nicholas. "Come on back, girls."

"We'd better beat it," Al said. "I don't like what's going on."

"Yes, come on, Terry. Let's go," said one of the younger youths.

"What do you know about Jim Morgan?" Nicholas asked Terry.

"Don't say," shouted Al, but too late because the girl had already said, "Terry's Jim Morgan's nephew."

"So that's it," thought James. "That began it all. That's why they've been so awful."

"What a revelation," said Nicholas.

Bromwyn was banging on the kiosk door. "It's urgent! Please come out, please!"

"All right, Missy. All right, in a moment. . . ."

"A moment will be too late."

Car lights were coming down the road. "Stop a minute," called a voice. It was a police car.

"They're on the common, aren't they?" shouted Daniel, leaning out of a window; then the police car went on. Fully a minute passed before Bromwyn realised that her job had been done for her. By this time the man was out of the kiosk.

"Thought you were in a hurry," he said.

"I was, but I'm not now." Limply, she began to walk back along the road, while he shrugged his shoulders, mounted a bicycle and pedalled away.

She could hear shouting on the common. The night had come to life. There was a roar of a motor-bike and she thought, "One has got away – which one? I've missed all the fun if there was any fun, and Daniel got the police there first. Where was he? How did he do it?"

Stirred by curiosity she started to run. The voices grew louder and she could recognise some of them before she turned the last corner and saw the common, the sand-dunes beyond and the sea dark, except where it was touched by the moon, when it was a shimmering silver gold.

Everything was over when Bromwyn reached the common. A policeman was taking notes from Nicholas and James, while three youths and two girls sat in the patrol car. A constable was examining the motor-bikes, while Anne and Stella were re-tethering the ponies.

"Hullo," Daniel said. "Bad luck about that man being in the kiosk. I was just telling Stella about it. Wouldn't he come out ?"

"No. He was beastly really. How did you know about them being here?"

"I was half a mile away with a pair of binoculars. I heard the motor-bikes. I couldn't see much. But I knew there were people on the common. I started to come this way and met the patrol car," Daniel replied scratching his nose. "It's happened just in time for me. I've got to go back to London tomorrow. Stella, will you come and stay with us? We live in Knightsbridge. It's awfully stuffy but, if you don't know London very well, it's not too bad."

"Well, they're properly caught now, Anne," Ivor said.

"We'll see your mates tomorrow," the constable told the youths in the car and the girl friends. "You can come along to the station now for a few more questions, and I shall want to see your licences and insurance."

"Have you got all of our addresses?" Nicholas asked.

"Yes, I think so. We can get in touch with you if we want to know any more. Can we take the camera along with us, Missy?"

Jocelyn stepped forward with her father's camera. "Yes; it's Daddy's but I'm sure he won't mind you having it," she said.

"Can the vet give a report on the condition of your

mare when he saw her the next day, Mr. Owen?" the Inspector asked Nicholas who was longing for a cigarette now that everything seemed over.

"Oh yes, I'm sure he can. His name is Mr. Harling. He hangs out by the station."

"Well, the best place for you now is bed, I think," the Inspector said.

The patrol car drove away; the motor-bikes still lay like fallen gods of speed on the common.

"Well, that's it," said Nicholas. "I'm exhausted."

"We caught them without a fight, except for Jocelyn. Are you all right, Jo?" asked James.

"You were wonderful, Jocelyn. I never thought I'd see you standing up and calmly taking photographs like that," said Nicholas.

"Perhaps the court will make them pay damages to Audrey," suggested Ivor, and now he wished that Maria could have been there too. "What about Maria's neck? I reckon they should pay for that too," he said grimly.

"We can start thinking about Dobbin and the church fête. Did you see something in the paper the other day about a pleasure-boat outfit wanting a barge horse? Do you think he would do for that? We can't keep him for ever can we?" asked Anne.

"I don't see why not."

"I'll write about him then."

"Now I want to settle down and enjoy the summer," said Bromwyn.

They could all hear a church clock now striking midnight. The beach below was quite empty now, though full of shadows.

"I'm going to stay with Daniel in London," Stella said.

"Where is he?" asked James.

"He's gone."

"I'm not surprised. He's probably locked out of the Grand as it is."

"You know he really saved the day. Another minute, and they would have fled," Anne said.

"But we still had the photographs," James replied.

"Yes, if they come out," answered Nicholas.

"It's all over now I suppose. It's sad, isn't it? I mean life will seem so dull now," said James. As they were about to part, Audrey met them in a big sweater, jeans and Wellington boots.

"I was about to visit you; then I met the police car. Jolly good! Congratulations! I'm going to reward you all with a free ride on Monday, a picnic one. I'll put everyone else off. Can you all come?" she asked.

"Can we?" exclaimed James.

"I should say so," said Stella.

"What about Daniel?" asked Audrey.

"He's going home tomorrow," Stella said. "But I think he will be back again. Perhaps he'll stay with Mummy and me."

"We can wait till then," Audrey said. "Well, you had better hurry home; this is no hour for children to be afoot. Don't speak to strangers, don't accept lifts."

"We know all that. It's been drummed into us from infancy," James interrupted.

"Well, thank you all over again."

"What sort of sentence will they get?" Bromwyn asked.

"Probably probation; but they'll know if they do it again it'll be a remand home, approved school or prison and that should stop them."

"One of them is a relation of Jim Morgan's. That must have sparked off something," Nicholas said.

"I hope it's only probation. I don't suppose they're really all that bad," said Ivor.

"Well, be at the stables by eleven on Monday. Bring sandwiches," Audrey said, turning into the stable-yard. "Now go on, scram."

"Well, good-bye all," Ivor said. "I'd better go. I'll

probably get in a row as it is; but I'm glad I was there; I wouldn't have missed it for anything."

"Good-bye, Ivor. See you Monday."

"Good-bye."

"Good-bye."

The sea still shimmered beneath the moon. James wanted to run down over the rocks and dance on the sand, the lovely, golden, moonlit sand.

"Come on, Jocelyn," he said, "we'd better run."

"Not again. I'm not going to," she answered. "I'm tired even if you aren't."

"I bet Maria's watching for us, Stella," Bromwyn said.

"You're telling me," Anne agreed.

The cottage looked ghostly with scaffolding on one side. Bits of sacking flapped on setting concrete; a piece of newspaper fluttered among the hollyhocks.

"Hullo. Come on then, what happened?" cried Maria as Bromwyn opened the back door.

"Ssh, don't shout. We caught them," Anne said.

Only Ivor's mother was waiting for him, nodding in the old armchair in the kitchen. "You're back then at last," she said.

"The police came. That gang – they won't go riding Audrey's ponies again," Ivor began.

Nicholas didn't mind so much about Trombone now. Some time during the night his anger had died. He was content to wait now until next holidays to ride seriously. He would spend the week-end at home, and on Monday there would be the picnic ride.

The lights were on at the Manse when he reached it. He took the keys of the padlocks on the stable door off the dresser in the kitchen. Another night had nearly gone; but it was a successful night this time; he didn't feel tired at all. Trombone whinnied when she heard his footsteps. By the light of the moon, he undid the padlocks.

"That's better isn't it? You'll be all right now, Trombone. They won't come again, not ever. You can grow fat and round and lazy and next holidays I'll start getting you fit. Perhaps in the spring we can compete in a one-day event together," he told his grey mare, with one arm round her neck, while her mane tickled his face.

"All the riding-school gang were wonderful tonight," he thought. "Even Jocelyn. And Daniel, well, he looks hopeless with his big nose and silly way of walking, but I suppose looks are not much of a criterion when it comes to judging people; he certainly made the grade tonight."

He heard a window flung up; light flooded the yard.

"Nicholas, is that you?" his mother called.

"Coming, Ma, coming," he called back. "Goodnight, Trombone."

He turned towards the house, thinking, "Really these hols haven't been too bad so far in spite of everything. And there's still a lot of them left. Even if I can't ride, there will still be plenty to do in one way or another.

"All the same I wish we had had a proper fight with the gang on motor-bikes," he thought, going upstairs. "It was a bit tame the way they gave up when the police came, except for the ones who bolted. We should have caught them; but somehow it was all over so soon. The police car came, we all stared at it, they were gone. Oh well, they'll be brought to justice just the same so it really doesn't matter. The battle's over and won," thought Nicholas.

It was too late now to switch on his radio. Records would waken his parents. He could only go to bed, but at least tonight he felt content; if it was still night, which he doubted, for once again the light was changing, another day beginning.

PONY BOOKS are very popular with boys and girls.
Dragon Books have a fine selection by the best authors to choose from:

JUMP TO THE STARS	Gillian Baxter	50p	☐
THE DIFFICULT SUMMER	Gillian Baxter	50p	☐
THE PERFECT HORSE	Gillian Baxter	60p	☐
SUE'S CIRCUS HORSE	Judith Berrisford	50p	☐
PONIES ALL SUMMER	Judith Berrisford	50p	☐
PONY FOREST ADVENTURE	Judith Berrisford	50p	☐
TROUBLE AT PONYWAYS	Judith Berrisford	50p	☐
SILVER BRUMBY'S KINGDOM	Elyne Mitchell	50p	☐
SILVER BRUMBIES OF THE SOUTH	Elyne Mitchell	50p	☐
SILVER BRUMBY	Elyne Mitchell	50p	☐
SILVER BRUMBY'S DAUGHTER	Elyne Mitchell	50p	☐
MY FRIEND FLICKA PART 1	Mary O'Hara	60p	☐
MY FRIEND FLICKA PART 2	Mary O'Hara	60p	☐
GREEN GRASS OF WYOMING 1	Mary O'Hara	40p	☐
GREEN GRASS OF WYOMING 2	Mary O'Hara	40p	☐
GREEN GRASS OF WYOMING 3	Mary O'Hara	40p	☐
THUNDERHEAD 1	Mary O'Hara	40p	☐
THUNDERHEAD 2	Mary O'Hara	40p	☐
THUNDERHEAD 3	Mary O'Hara	40p	☐

All these books are available at your local bookshop or newsagent, or can be ordered direct from the publisher. Just tick the titles you want and fill in the form below.

Name ....

Address ....

....

Write to Dragon Cash Sales, PO Box 11, Falmouth, Cornwall TR10 9EN. Please enclose remittance to the value of the cover price plus: UK: 18p for the first book plus 8p per copy for each additional book ordered to a maximum charge of 66p. BFPO and EIRE: 18p for the first book plus 8p per copy for the next 6 books, thereafter 3p per book. OVERSEAS: 20p for the first book and 10p for each additional book.
Granada Publishing reserve the right to show new retail prices on covers, which may differ from those previously advertised in the text or elsewhere.